On Becoming You

You Are a Powerful Being of
Light, All is Within You

Kathi Pickett

BALBOA.
PRESS

A DIVISION OF HAY HOUSE

Balboa Press books may be ordered through booksellers or by contacting:

Balboa Press
A Division of Hay House
1663 Liberty Drive
Bloomington, IN 47403
www.balboapress.com
1 (877) 407-4847

Print information available on the last page.

ISBN: 978-1-9822-2824-8 (sc)
ISBN: 978-1-9822-2826-2 (hc)
ISBN: 978-1-9822-2825-5 (e)

Library of Congress Control Number: 2019906859

Balboa Press rev. date: 06/04/2019

This book is dedicated to my dearest parents for a lifetime of
unconditional love and support—
Jane Alvina Rieth Meyers and Garry William Moore Meyers

Contents

Introduction

Have you ever thought, *I do everything for everyone else and there is never time for me, I don't have enough money, my job is boring, I don't know how I got where I am in life, my body is out of shape, and my life is stressful*? I just want peace in my life. This may be the most important journey that you will ever take—a journey to discover and embody your true nature and expand your perception beyond what you can see, feel, taste, smell, and touch.

My journey began as a child playing and traveling with beings of light. I remember sitting on a beach and looking up at clouds as the beings of light appeared. I curiously observed these air-like beings who wore long, flowing, white gowns of glowing light. Their movements were fluid, effortless, and weightless. The next thing I knew I would be flying effortlessly among the clouds with the beings of light by my side. We would laugh and sing.

The welcoming beings of light mesmerized me. I soaked in their indescribable essence as though I was basking in the warmth of the sun. I did not need instruction. My experiences seemed familiar, as though I had been with them before. I had no fear as some may expect because the air-like beings of light filled me with a pure essence of unconditional love, grace, and peace.

My first adventures with the beings of light came after a near-drowning experience in the summer before I turned four years old. I will tell this story in detail in the first chapter.

I was drawn to understand these beings of light. Were they dead people, I wondered, or angels? I studied death and dying and read Elisabeth Kubler-Ross in college. I visited the first hospice in America, established in Branford, Connecticut, in 1974. I visited in 1975, when I was nineteen years old, to learn firsthand how to die with dignity in a comfortable home setting.

For decades, the light beings' subtle, soft voices in my head guided me as a nurse to support patients and families to move gracefully through transitions at the end of life. They were all my teachers. The beings of light reminded me of the universal truths that I already knew. I was curious and therefore open to receive their information. I felt at one in my mind, body, and soul during these experiences.

As an adult raising a family, I had a busy, productive life that included graduate school, full-time work, raising children, and juggling a few too many activities. My oldest son dropped out of high school and joined the Marines. He left for Parris Island in the midst of a layoff at work and a challenging career transition. My second son floundered and lived at home. My husband embraced his passion to stay home and day trade, which led to financial stress and more anxiety.

My external life and the interior of my soul became fractured. I did not communicate with the beings of light. I felt separate from my true self, but who was I? My health and vitality dwindled due to a debilitating illness of frequent migraines, vertigo, and depression. I was in crisis, often asking myself, *How did this happen to me?* and *How did I end up here?* I felt like I was in a snow globe that had just been shaken up.

Headaches and vertigo limited my ability to enjoy life. An obligatory stillness was required to quiet the pain, while nausea and dizziness limited by ability to attend family functions, social activities, and work and to be fully present for my teenage sons.

One Sunday morning while drinking tea and eating dry toast, I fell to the floor. I could not stand or speak; I was physically unable to move my legs. I was taken to the emergency room in an ambulance as my bewildered son looked on. I was helpless and thought that I had had a stroke. The physicians determined I had a severe migraine, gave me intravenous medications, and sent me home, after which my speech and motor functions returned. Two days later, I again fell to the floor, motionless and unable to speak or stand. Twelve days in the hospital yielded no answers; Western medicine was stumped. A realization settled in: I was on my own to heal. But how? I had no resources.

The external world of medicine, family, and friends could not heal me.

I sensed that a shift in my life was required. Through stillness and deep meditation, I connected to the interior world of my true essence to find my way home to myself. During the stillness, the soft, quiet voices of the beings of light returned to offer advice. It was then, deep inside, I knew that I was shaken awake by a force beyond my physical body.

My spiritual transformation took a major leap forward. My experiences from early in life led me to feel safe and adept in the nonphysical realms. I came to believe that I had past lives and that lessons from these lives were accessible to me. I explored many past lives, developed intuition, honed energy-healing skills, and received many teachings from spirit guides and wise teachers in the physical world. Through these rich teachings I was able to open my heart, build confidence, and release doubt, fear, and shame to heal myself—as well as to become me.

Amid an oscillating, tumultuous life, I found peace and happiness with guidance from my spirit allies. As I cleared out the clutter in my mind, I became more clairvoyant and clairsentient, weaving me through a series of mystical experiences.

Before long, I became aware that I was still communicating with souls, as I had when I was young. Only now I was able to accurately interpret information from both living and deceased souls. As the word spread of my abilities, more and more people sought out a session with me. I was encouraged by family and friends to pursue a private practice. Decades as an experienced professional nurse had prepared me for my healing-energy practice. My intuition became stronger the more I intentionally used it and received affirmative feedback from clients.

The more I knew, the more positively I was able to provide life changing feedback to help clients. It was then, I devoted myself to my healing practice, and continued my studies, which included taking many workshops and classes, reading dozens of books, studying with master healers, and listening to my spirit guides. I discovered many modalities that support healing through an understanding of energy medicine.

I studied healing with sound, crystals, essential oils, reiki, healing touch, angels, and so much more. Caroline Myss, Anodea Judith, Cyndi Dale, Mark Earlix, and Juelle were master teachers on earth whose podcasts, books, and seminars were invaluable to me. After thousands of healing energy sessions, I realized that reducing stress was the key to healing. And the key to reducing stress is a daily practice to balance the energy system.

After a decade or more, I was well on my way as a healer; my life was balanced and predictable. My children found their way in the world, two beautiful granddaughters were born, we had frequent celebrations with our close-knit, extended family, we lived in a lovely home on the side of a mountain, and I had many dear friends and a husband who supported me emotionally and financially. I felt happy and blessed to embrace my vocation to speak, write, and practice as an intuitive healing energy practitioner.

Then one day a lightning bolt flashed across the scene of my life, when my husband announced he had been in an intimate relationship with another woman. I found myself moving out of my house to live alone. It was better than fighting with my husband while he entertained himself with his new life and friend. I was brought to my knees in despair, paralyzed, and unable to abide or alter my fate. Where was my strength, the stamina I had held for so long and taught so effectively to others?

My vision for living out my life with my partner of thirty-seven years now seemed unlikely. Profound disappointment in love and bitter feelings prevailed. How could this be happening to me? Not being able to process the magnitude of the changes in my life, my emotions ran out of control and exhaustion set in.

Chaos entered my life uninvited. I knew from my energy medicine studies that there are many layers and pockets of memories and experiences buried within the fabric of our being. I wondered if there was a reason for this chaos that I would discover deep within my psyche. Was there a part of me that needed to be seen, heard, and loved? What was I supposed to be healing? A monster of jealousy, anger, and rage had filled my body in place of love. I was losing my grip. How could I manage a single lifestyle after all these years? What would I lose? What would I gain? It took time to see my truth and to stand in my power.

Through prayer, spiritual practice, and the power of choosing to love the world, I was swept along to a period of feeling safe and content. The commencement of a period of inspired creativity nurtured by family and friends' kindnesses fostered a light heart, emotional contentment, and creative expression, and soon a gladness to be alive prevailed. And thus, I moved from chaos to clarity to self-empowerment, and you can too!

You cannot see the emotions, the thoughts, or the memories that affect the subatomic particles moving beneath the story of your life. An understanding of the universal energy laws gave me the context to better understand and affect my physical, emotional, mental, and spiritual health. You may feel overwhelm, dread, fear, or anxiety, which are invisible to the eye. Tuning into the subtle current of energy of these emotions combined with an understanding of the energy and mystical laws can give form to that which is invisible and, thus, solutions to heal.

Only a spark is needed to ignite an expression of the latent treasures within you that became dormant while you were living a busy, productive, and often stressful life. You have a rich resource within your heart to heal yourself and others. As in my life, when you ignore or refuse to listen to this inner wisdom, it can lead to fear, loss, confusion, and suffering.

By reading this book, you will learn the processes to gain personal power and a deeper understanding of how it all fits together with the energy and mystical laws to heal, manifest, and transform your life.

- You will learn the mechanics of the energy system and the tools to foster health and vibrancy.
- You will heal through processes and tools that awaken you to your true nature.
- You will learn to invoke the nature of our highly structured, impersonal universe to create synchronicities, magic, and miracles.

On Becoming You invites you to find rhythm in your life and enjoy the life you were meant to live. Through story, mysteries are unraveled in a clear language to provide new insights and knowledge that can be woven into your life. I will inspire you to embrace new beginnings, to release inevitable endings, and to ignite a transformation on becoming you. It is your time!

Your spirit is an invisible aspect of you, albeit the most important. Your spirit interacts with the forces of nature, the spirit world, and the universe at large. This nonphysical reality of spirit can be accessed through intuition, spirit guides, and an understanding of the energy and mystical laws. *On Becoming You* is an instructional guide to connecting with one's own spirituality and eternal place in the universe. As your guide, I teach tools to connect with your intuition, spirit guides, higher power, and the universe. You need support to unlock the mysteries and the truths held in the fabric of your being and to learn the tools to keep you on track. This book will do both.

There is no reason good enough not to be the best you that you can be. This book is about loving yourself to become who you were meant to be. It is time to relax, enjoy, and smile. You are on your way.

PART 1
A Nonphysical Reality

On Becoming You
is a window into the energy and mystical realms
of magic and possibilities
seen through my initiations as a child, an
adult, and an intuitive energy healer.

CHAPTER 1
A Beginning

Seeing is believing, right? What do you believe? Most people have had experiences that could not be explained in terms of physical reality, especially when they were children. I invite you to recall a time you knew something to be true without evidence, such as a child who figures out that Santa's not real despite no one's having told him or her yet. Or was there a time you sensed the presence of a deceased loved one or an angel? Perhaps you had a dream about someone or something that came true. The subconscious holds an innate ability to connect with more than we can see.

My First Memory of Beings of Light

On a hot midsummer day in Key West, Florida, when I was almost four, my two older sisters and I gingerly walked over sharp coral and broken shells that spattered the sand between our home and the water's edge. We were careful not to scratch our soft bodies. Occasional sprigs of grass that somehow survived the harsh conditions of sun, salt water, and lack of soil were not enough to offer a path for our bare feet, and our thin rubber flip-flops often fell off. We had to scrunch up our toes to keep them on.

My sisters, my friends, and I often walked in the water when it was low tide to get to a sandbar on the opposite shore. The water would rise several feet and bring the tide water, large fish, and small sharks through this narrow channel. Even at a young age, I loved adventure and a challenge. On this day, as usual, we needed to get back before the tide came in.

In the fifties, when it was time for dinner, you were expected to be home on time, washed, and ready to eat. But I was easily distracted and played too long. My sisters had already arrived on the shore near our home and were calling for me to hurry, so I headed to the shore. My feet did not touch the bottom. The incoming tide was moving fast and threw me off balance. I lost my flip-flops and began to dog paddle. I panicked as my bare feet touched the swaying sea grass, afraid that a shark might be near. The brackish seawater tasted awful. I spit it out and ended up swallowing more. Clumsily, I bobbed up and down in the water, making forward movement toward my sisters on the shore. In my confused state, I could see them moving toward our two-story flat, which helped to guide me.

In a daze, guided by my sisters, I walked up the stairs and ate dinner, and then we all got in the bathtub together. The next thing I knew, I was floating above and in the scene at the same time. I was not in my body; I could see my body below. I sensed beings of light, or angels, all around me. Where was I really? I remember being apprehensive at first, not even knowing if the beings of light could speak or if I should speak. I just observed and soaked in a sense of well-being. The air-like beings of light welcomed me with the pure essence of unconditional love. I sensed that I was filled with brilliant light. I had no body—I became an illuminated light being too with a sense of no longer being bound to earth. I was in a dream-like state.

In my mind, the air-like beings of light appeared to be wearing long, flowing, white gowns of light. They communicated without audible words. I simply knew what they were thinking. They showed me the scene I had just experienced. I was crying, choking, and coughing up the brackish seawater, exhausted from fear and struggling in the water. Had I almost drowned? They assured me that I was not going to die and that the water was safe, saying I just had to be careful next time. They were loving and kind, with no judgment or criticism.

I hesitated to return to my family. The beings of light said, "You belong on earth. We love you and will always be with you. You can visit anytime." I felt safe, comforted, blissful, and enveloped in pure love and happiness. I never questioned where I was; it did not have a location. Was it within me or beyond me or beyond this world? I didn't know; I simply accepted.

I was delirious and not aware of where I was when I first returned to full consciousness, no longer in a dream-like state. In what seemed like a split second, I was getting out of the tub wrapped in a towel, ready to head off to bed.

Every night my sisters and I knelt together and prayed, "God bless Mommy, Daddy, Bridget, Mary, Kathleen, Brenda, Aileen, Grandma and Grandpa Rieth, Aunt Barbara, Aunt MaryAnn, Uncle Gerald, Janet, Debbie, Lisa, Michele, Uncle Leo, Aunt Theresa, Patty, Tommy, Terry, Grandma and Grandpa Perkins, Ida, Beth and Phil, and all our loved ones." This nightly blessing of family had significance beyond a perfunctory ritual. We expressed gratitude for one another. We would never be alone. We would always be loved and cared for by our family.

As a young child not yet four years of age, I accepted the visit from the beings of light as normal and natural. The memory of this exquisite experience was replayed in my mind over and over. The feeling of bliss was enticing. I would return to this state safely in my dreams as I gained my comfort in transitioning between these worlds of existence. Once I was more fluid with the transitions, I became adept at crossing back and forth between the physical and nonphysical worlds in my waking states, eventually without an escort from the beings of light.

Childhood

As a child, I always felt loved, cared for, and never alone. Mine was a military family, and we moved frequently as a merry band of travelers, our own community of seven. Our relocations led to a series of transitions and new starts. My mother always assured me, "If you made friends in one place, then wherever we go, you will make new friends. There are good people everywhere." This lesson would prove valuable throughout my life, with every transition and change fortifying my confidence that all was well. Every new school and neighborhood excited me. I learned about myself in all the newness.

My parents took us to church and catechism to learn that God loves us, to follow the Ten Commandments, to say our prayers of the Our Father and Hail Mary, to share our blessings with those less fortunate, and to see the light of God in everyone. My Catholic upbringing fostered a strong belief in God. We had saints in the invisible world—Saint Anthony to find lost objects, Saint Christopher for protection when we traveled, and many more. Our angels were always with us, and just as the sun shone everywhere, God's love shone everywhere and was always with us. Faith in the unseen formed a foundation to believe in the nonphysical world and invisible beings. It seemed natural.

One day at a Catholic elementary school, I was dancing and singing with other children in a garden near the entrance to our school. Our skirts flew out wide around our little bodies as we circled a statue of Mother Mary. It was magical and exhilarating. My energy was exuberant. Sister Veronica said, "You are being disruptive and disrespectful. This is a sacred garden and not to play in." In my rapture, I kept dancing even when the sisters told me to stop. I defended myself, saying, "Mother Mary was pleased, and what about the other children?"

Apparently, no one saw the other children. My punishment was to stand in the hallway with my nose in a chalk-drawn circle on the wall. Self-consciously, I stared directly at the wall, hoping no one would recognize me. I thought that because we all wore the same uniform, we all looked the same from behind. I hoped that no one would know that it was me standing there humiliated.

I realized I was different and learned not to tell people about seeing the beings of light. They seemed so real to me that I could not fathom that others could not see them.

As a voracious reader, I spent hours gobbling up books, such as *Charlotte's Web, A Snowy Day, A Blue Dolphin*, and *A Wrinkle in Time*. As a child, I would imagine I was in the stories and flying around the world. I assumed I had a good imagination. Now I wonder if something else was really happening. Was I really traveling?

I enjoyed stretching my mind and seeing the world. I was one of those kids who would sneak under the covers at night with a flashlight to finish a book or spend recess time reading. When I was not reading, I was drawing. I carried a drawing pad with me and drew objects and scenes. I was not a great artist, but I enjoyed capturing my world. I would clear my mind and focus on an object I intended to draw. As I focused on each object, I would sense its essence in order to recreate it on paper. I would feel tingling in my hands as my energy shifted to that of the object. I did not feel separate from the tree, flower, plane, or landscape. In some invisible energetic exchange, waves of light would move through me to the paper.

In my large, military, Catholic family, rules encased in love created structure and conformity. I would be told to use my inside voice when running in from outside to exclaim some newfound wonder in nature. We were told to not ask questions when told to do something—just do it. Questioning the way things were done or why was considered talking back to my parents. We were taught to obey authority without question and to control our emotions so we could listen to our own good judgment. Good and bad behavior were reinforced at home and school. If you were good, you were rewarded; if you were bad, you could be punished. It was difficult to learn to trust my own inner guidance with so many rules.

I kept my experiences with beings of light and deceased souls to myself to avoid conflict or confrontation. As Catholics, my family believed in saints and the Holy Spirit but not in seeing dead people. My sisters did not believe me and would say that I was making it up. The undertone was that I wanted attention. I began pruning my purest expression. Beneath the surface of my being resided a do-not-fence-me-in rebel who wanted to be as free as wildflowers.

During my adolescent years, when movies portrayed spirits as evil, I pushed ghosts away, sending them into my closet and closing the door. At the time, I was not sure how it worked, but they got the message. I was petrified—the spirits of dead people were not the warm, comforting beings of light I was used to seeing. I shut off my ability in an effort to stop the visitations. I never told anyone about the nightmares and spirits that came calling.

Even a mildly scary movie would give me nightmares for days, weeks, or months. My interior was important and needed protection. I refused to watch scary movies. I had no intention of acknowledging or engaging with horrors.

A Young Adult

I knew I wanted to help people even as a child—what a cliché, right? In the seventies, the common career choices for women were nurse, secretary, and teacher. I chose to go to college and graduated with a bachelor of science in nursing. We had a saying in college: "If it feels good, do it; if in doubt, get out." I trusted my intuition and relied on it as I became exposed to many situations that I had no experience to fall back on. "First, do no harm" and "Always be safe" were rules to live by. My sophomore year I lived in an Intentional Democratic Community (IDC) on campus, a commune based on the behaviorist principles of B. F. Skinner's book *Walden Two*. It was while learning the credit system of governance, cleaning, cooking, and appointing our living spaces that I learned about the nature of community living.

My sisters and parents lived in several states, including Massachusetts, Connecticut, Tennessee, and Texas. My sense of adventure led me to live in a commune, travel cross country, and backpack across Ireland. I continued to embrace reading, painting, racquetball, snowshoeing, skiing, and hiking. An overwhelming sense of adventure and the lack of roots in a geographical location led me to travel and explore new lifestyles.

A close friend knew someone from the IDC who also wanted to go cross country. She trusted him, so I trusted him and off we went. We were both carefree and easygoing. I had seen most of the East Coast growing up, so I went west and southwest. We traveled cross country for several months camping in national parks in the central, western, and southwestern United States. I took with me only what I absolutely needed as I headed out wide-eyed, off to see the world. Without routines, stuff, a job, or commitments, I was free to be me. When my trip was complete, I had been to a total of forty-two states, enjoying hiking and meeting people from around the country. We had shared stories around campfires at night that reinforced that we are more alike than different.

I was free to learn who am I and had rarely stayed in the same place more than a night. I had not taken a camera with me on this four-month-long trip. I thought each day's experience would melt into me and become part of the fabric of who I am. I would not need a picture because this trip would become me. I was twenty-two years old and naïve—boy, do I wish I had just one picture from that trip.

I had an awakening during my travels. The nightly blessing prayer came back to me. I will never forget when this awareness flowed over me like a wave of comfort from my head to my toes: "You are not alone." It was not an audible voice but was strong and clear. I sensed my family's presence inside of me. This sense of an emotional bond across time and space was a revelation. Our geographical distance does not matter; we are still one as a family. The timing of this revelation was opportune, giving me confidence for a series of new starts in Nashville, Tennessee, and then Dallas, Texas.

I found a job quickly at Vanderbilt Pediatrics in Nashville, where I learned the true joy and pain of caring for terminally ill children and their parents during a time of immense loss. My daily routine was being present, crying with, holding, and breathing with families. I felt blessed to be of service. My ability to experience the beings of light prepared me to see the light in each of these children. I could connect with their divine light and observe them outside of their bodies.

I was with countless children as they received chemotherapy and appeared to be in a coma but were happily playing with deceased loved ones, angels, or children in the Other World. They would return to their bodies once the toxins had cleared and the side effects were more tolerable.

As with the beings of light, communication among the children's divine lights was effortless. The children's divine lights would ask me to talk to their parents when it was time for them to transition. One six-year-old boy said, "Tell my mom to let me go. I am okay, really. I want to be free. This is no life for me, or for her. Look at my body—this is not who I want to be, all bloated and fat. I cannot even move anymore. Tell her I will always love her and be near." It took courage to tell families what I had heard from their children's divine lights. The messages were so clear and comforting, though, that in time I learned to trust my inner guidance system. And the families were always so grateful. My presence at transitions was purposeful work. I could be in both worlds at the same time, creating a sacred space for all.

In my mind's eye, I would also see elderly patients with dementia, some tied to their beds for safety, appear as divine light and roaming around free as birds, visiting family members and entertaining themselves on the earthly plane. It is clear to me that our spirits are eternal and that our divine lights are powerful and not limited to the physical body. The children in the hospital were my teachers.

As beautiful as these experiences were, I became entangled by a desire to raise a family, build a career, and appoint a home. Responsibilities and ambition in the physical realm had my full attention.

I fell in love, got married, and started raising a family within two years. My mind attached fiercely to why I should have what I want and where, why, when, and how it should be. I wanted financial security and a place to call home, and it took money, time, a strong work ethic, and discipline to manage my money. I wanted it all now, and the home should be well appointed in a good neighborhood with good schools. The thought perseverated like a washing machine stuck on the spin cycle, and then disappointment set in. I did not have patience and lacked the ability to fully see my blessings. I decided to power through by working excessive hours and adding more to my plate to make all the pieces fit. My temperament resisted, and the lack of flow in my life led to high blood pressure, migraines, stress, irritability, and poor health.

The freedom to fill my spirit with the lusciousness of nature and to schedule unencumbered family moments and time with gracious, caring friends seemed less and less available. There were only so many hours in a day, and my days were tightly scheduled. There was less time for prayer, meditation, and stillness, or so the reasoning mind assumed.

An episode of depression set in when I left Dallas for New England in financial despair while raising my young children. Depression led me to wonder, *Who is that crazy person who complains, feels sorry for herself, and seems barred from a happy life?* Self-limiting thoughts circled round and round in my head, creating a stuck feeling, an inertia too severe to escape.

Within a year of moving to New England, I was thrilled that our third child would be born into a healthy, stable family, a blessing after so much disruption in Dallas. During an ultrasound at four months gestation, I said to my mother, who had accompanied me to my appointment, "Look! She is waving at us, saying hello." A few days after Christmas—in slow motion so that I had ample time to really see her—she floated buoyantly over my bed, waving. It wasn't until the end of the week that I knew she had been saying good-bye.

I could not understand how a benevolent God or health-care community would not intervene. My uterus was thin, and a specialist was required. The only fetal demise and abortion specialist in the hospital system was on vacation. This further sickened me.

I isolated myself from family and friends and did not seek medical or therapeutic assistance. I questioned whether there was a God; if I was being punished; and if I was weak, stupid, or just incapable of a successful life. The beauty and joy in my life evaded me while I focused on what was wrong and needed to be fixed. I was hard on myself.

I said to myself, "My womb is a tomb. My womb is a tomb," as I was sobbing, unable to eat, and throwing up when I did force some food down. I felt a cold, empty stillness throughout my body. I knew her spirit was not there. I was not even sure I was still alive because the stillness was so cold, deep, and penetrating. After four days, I delivered the physical remains of my baby. The autopsy revealed a perfect baby girl. The doctor told me, "A million things have to go right. Her heart just stopped."

Everywhere I went, I saw pregnant women and small babies. I isolated myself at home. My abdomen still showed the baby bulge, and retelling the story to acquaintances in town was too tiring. There were no answers. Why did my baby die? I felt like a victim. Was I being punished? I felt ashamed. Was there something wrong with me? I could not accept this loss. Why me? A deep, dark depression enveloped me. I was trapped in a cycle that I could not break.

I wish I had known where to go for support to heal. I did not trust the health-care community, therapists, or priests. I felt alone on my journey. I went through the motions of life, secretly crying too often. I avoided work as a nurse, deciding instead to make quilts and find stores to sell them. My family deserved more of me; I deserved more of me. Beneath the surface of my life, my soul began to stir.

One day, my spirit was ignited. I studied art, color theory, and quilting techniques with masters. My thoughts and emotions naturally quieted in communion with the silence of the process, and I found peace within. I entered several juried shows and won ribbons. Art consultants sold and exhibited my work in galleries in several states.

In union with my soul, each piece was a one-of-a-kind creation. Deep emotions that were rotting in my stomach dissipated with my shift in focus. Hope and gratitude embedded in the colors, textures, stitches, and designs of every piece. I became enveloped in the moment, the past dissolved, and I loved myself more each day. As a sense of peace and connectedness fell over me, I healed from the inside out.

As it often happens when I clear my mind and emotions, I am more open to the spirit world. Soon to follow I had a visit in a meditation from a soul that did not come to earth, the daughter who had died. In meditation,

I was in complete stillness as a vision of a very active young girl came to me. I was not clear on exactly what she was doing, but she appeared to be very busy. I could sense that she was smart and confident with red hair and a strong body. She told me that she was the soul of my baby who had died. With a clear, crisp voice, she said, "You would have your hands full with two sons, and another child would be too much. Not to worry; all is well." Her spirit was light and breezy, almost effervescent in nature—maybe even flighty. It was as though changing her mind about coming to earth as my daughter was no big deal. This brief conversation led to a deeper healing. I trusted that her soul was alive and well.

Just as chaos had entered my life, a dormant life force sprouted out of the blue through meditation and prayer. The strength of my divine light emerged. It was as though a daffodil had broken through the ground after a long winter's rest, and a wave of hope lifted me. Within weeks, this sense of life rising up inside of me led to creative expression, a proof of life.

My passion for quilting led to a commissioned art quilt for a local Visiting Nurse Association (VNA), which ignited my desire to return to nursing. I became a maternal child health nurse and a certified sudden infant death counselor, helping families grieve the loss of their infants. Mothers appreciated my perspective on life, the afterlife, and the value of living their lives to the fullest.

My process to heal came through creative expression, quietude, reflection, connecting to my essence, affirmation of the afterlife, and acknowledging that a soul is waiting in the wings to be born on its schedule. I felt alive with meaningful work as a nurse and mother. I released my grief in losing a child to help others heal.

I realized I had to change something in my life, but I was not sure what to do. I decided to pray and withdraw from superfluous activities that added to the confusion. My emotions settled. All it took was a crack, an opening, to create an awareness that if I wanted to live a full, meaningful life, I had to help myself. This clarity allowed my spirit to ascend as though a rocket of light was being shot out from my heart. The universe responded, and with a leap of faith I could see the beauty in the world and enjoy my life.

This awakening was accompanied by an urgency to be whole and required a steady forward movement of effort and self-love. It became easier as I gained strength, fostering my growth. Eventually it gained enough momentum to propel me forward to an even richer state of awareness and joy. I went back to work as a nurse, found child care, and saved money. Within a year I owned a house on the side of a mountain. I felt as though I was on my way again and embraced my life.

All these experiences separated me from the beings of light and my true self, a condition that lasted years, which is way too long to not be aligned. I could not hold my power. The guidance from the beings of light was evasive, just out of reach. My overthinking mind and emotions got in the way. It was not clear to me how or what had happened to propel me forward in life as the depression lifted. It just happened as if by magic. I slowed down and reflected on my life and then made conscious choices to move forward.

The magic that happens beneath the surface of what we see in the physical world is always there. The lessons and experiences from childhood and adulthood teach us who we really are. Learn to embrace and reflect on the gift of knowledge and wisdom that you can glean from all your experiences. It is your life, and it is up to you to find its meaning. You are never alone.

Chapter 2
A Spiritual Crisis

A spiritual crisis can come when the world as you know it changes forever, and you will never be the same again. A spiritual crisis can be an initiation into the mystical world of magic and possibilities and begin with a life-changing event—an illness as in my case, a near-death experience, or an enlightening epiphany. My confidence and joy as a young adult led to a new home, a master's in business administration, a busy social calendar, children engaged in school and sports, and a happy time.

The magic that got me this far in my life dissolved without the support of self-care. I fell prey to the tug and pull of the external world. I had too much to do and not enough time. I powered through to meet demands at work and home and attended the frequent family events that come with a large family. My busy, productive life left little time for meditation and self-reflection.

Family life became stressful and challenged with financial constraints. My husband's income dropped significantly while he was day trading, and my career transition as a business analyst, my first position with a master's degree, was stressful. I was out of my element as a nurse for several decades, and the learning curve was steep and demanding. My teenage sons were challenging. The depths of the lows and the peaks of the highs kept me out of balance. I struggled to find peace in jogging, yoga, and too much wine. I chose to stuff down unresolved grief and powered through.

The dysfunction in my life took its toll on me. Who was I really? Who did I want to be? What was my purpose? At the time, I could not tell you except through my resume. The truth is that I was not living my life as me. Depression returned. I had survived such hard times—why now?

An initiation brewed over the past decade that led to my vocation as an energy healer and clairvoyant in the midnineties. I was plagued with frequent debilitating migraines and vertigo lasting several days, occurring more weeks out of the month than not. My blood pressure skyrocketed during these episodes, leaving its insalubrious trail in my vascular system and organs. Essential oils were soothing, while the other four senses demanded obligatory silence.

My sensory system needed absolute stillness—no sound, no light, no touch, no thoughts, no feelings—a clearing of my energy system. This malady of vertigo and headaches was relentlessly forcing me to retreat from family and friends. Was this a punishment for bad choices, for my mistakes? Why was this happening to me? Though I would call out to God, there would be no answer. My third serious clinical depression set in, and this time I sought help from Western medicine. There was no real help. I was given several medications that caused even worse side effects and pursued vestibular rehabilitation. I could not lean my head back to have my teeth cleaned or my hair washed at a salon without coming close to passing out. My life shrank.

During this time my finances were strapped, but since my career opportunities were escalating, I needed to be on track. Relentless disruptions with my children, who could not seem to get on their own two feet financially and relied on us for support, put commensurate pressure on my marriage and finances. The confusion and struggles in their lives made them unbalanced, and the hurt in my soul was deep. I was helpless. Together David and I sought a sanctuary; we bought a sailboat for pleasure and relaxation and spent most weekends on Buzzards Bay or Martha's Vineyard.

Jogging five miles several days during the week and spending the weekends on the boat were not enough to keep me in balance. I collapsed. My body failed me. An illness that affected my ability to walk in a straight line, to speak clearly, to form words or articulate my thoughts was never diagnosed. I was kept in the hospital for twelve days and transferred to Mass General for a neurological workup that yielded no answers.

In a dream-like state, I was a small girl inside a clay body who peered out of the sockets of the eyes. When the nurse conducted her admission assessment, I told her that Jimmy Carter was president and my name was

Kathi Meyers (my maiden name). From within my clay body, I looked around the room as though my eyes were begging for answers from my family. The nurse said she would come back later and try the questions again after I rested. *Why?* I thought. My sisters' eyes were expressionless, and their mouths fixed as they looked at me in disbelief. They were stunned and speechless at my demise.

Then, I realized that Jimmy Carter was not the president. I questioned myself, *Why can't I remember the man's name with the white hair?* I could not, even if my life had depended on it. In my mind I was a twenty-year-old single woman living in Connecticut—a gap of over twenty years. I was lost and scared. I knew my answers were not correct.

Frozen within my body in my hospital bed in silence, I listened to the colorful life memories of two brothers preparing to say good-bye to their comatose mother with dementia in the next bed. Day after day, they would arrive to tell stories to their mother, who listened in silence. They told the story of their father offering tomatoes to the hobos who lived under the bridge and family dinners with more food than anyone could eat. They meticulously described how to prepare eggplant and the secret to their mothers' sauce and the homemade wine.

I was a witness to their truths as they honestly recounted the wonder of their colorful lives. The stories were a healing for their mothers' transition. I felt blessed to be present. The tales of their rich lives filled with laughter and family gatherings helped me refocus on my life and my future too.

It was as though the motherboard in my brain was shutting down and wires were tangled. I tried sorting out my life and realized I did not have enough space in my head. I wanted to be airlifted out. "Just get me out of here!" I cried. Of course, it did not work; I was a mess and stuck. But I was grateful, that my husband came every day to see me even when I was in Boston. He was my anchor.

My speech would come and go with the intensity of the headache and vertigo. I was swinging between sanity and madness. A referral to psychology was next. A psychiatric resident asked me if I could leave my body. I thought, *What a strange question.* I wondered if she sensed, though unbeknownst to me, I was not in my body. Having nothing to lose, I told her that I could and that I used to meditate, but it had been a while. She suggested I meditate to see what happened. The neurologist told me, "Keep jogging and all will be well." These physicians were angels sent to deliver a message to me: "Go inside beyond the physical reality to find wholeness." The answers can only be found within.

Upon leaving the hospital, I had lost fifteen pounds and was able to walk less than a mile at a very slow speed. Why were my legs not working? For the next five weeks I had a very structured routine with three healthy meals a day, meditation, spiritual reading, walking on the treadmill, and no wine. I logged my slow and steady progress in a notebook.

My body craved light, so I would meditate in the sunlight and the moonlight to receive the rays reflected from the sun. During meditation in the absolute stillness of my mind, body, and emotions, I could easily embrace the beings of light as they filled me with light, love, and healing. In the stillness there is a silence that stretches from the floor to the ceiling and from wall to wall. The room is still and the air is still, yet in the stillness I could see infinite tiny particles of dust that I could not see before the light streamed in through the window. The dust reminded me that there is so much more that we cannot see. Then the room vanishes as I float into the nothingness of peace and calm.

During meditation a limitless sea of faces appeared; each drop in the sea was a lost soul seeking to communicate with me. The souls would all talk at once, pushing in front of one another to get close to me. The vision was similar to the *Beetlejuice* movie and the line of ghosts all battered and torn, seeking redemption or solace.

It became impossible to sleep or meditate without their intrusion— men, women, and children spanning hundreds of years, all with their own stories and requesting help. It reminded me of when I was an adolescent and the spirits would come at night and terrify me, and I made them go away. This time I decided that I would attempt to communicate with them to find out what they wanted. To my surprise, I could communicate with them as easily as the beings of light when I was a child.

A deceased soul might ask for me to tell their mother they are okay and to thank her for her love and support. Another may ask to be guided to the light for their ascension into the afterlife. I will tell you more on this in subsequent chapters. Of course, spirits have a range of personalities. I would have to learn how to protect myself and steer clear of the not-so-nice ones. The peaceful beings of light showed up and helped.

Many people told me that because I had this gift, I had to use it to help people grieve by connecting with their loved ones. I was not convinced that it was a gift or that a requirement existed that I provide such a service. There was much to learn about helping souls cross into the light and to communicate between worlds. I had a family and work obligations.

Deep inside I knew I had a choice to embrace this aspect of me or not. My spirit guides encouraged me, and I embraced the opportunity to be of service. To be able to transition souls through time and space and to reunite souls with deceased loved ones was an honor and a blessing that filled me with purpose. I found a sacred calling.

I wondered, what more there was to see. My heart answered, "There is more, always more, and then more and more." The universal consciousness, the *all* is infinite, beyond imagination.

My husband was skeptical. He heard me talking to the souls at night and screaming when caught off guard by their presence. My heart became determined to find peace and calm amid the souls coming to me. I was on a spiritual quest.

My roller coaster with depression, regret, and loss needed to be in the rear-view mirror. In order to smooth out my life and my rough edges I asked the spirit world for help. The beings of light would continue to whisper softly and gently to me, offering guidance to trust myself and quiet my mind and emotions to better hear my inner voice. They told me to go inside and follow my true essence. They described the universal mystical and energy laws that I will share in a later chapter. I never felt a sense of coercion or urgency from them. They comfortably drifted in and out of my awareness, weaving effortlessly through my life behind the scenes.

During a meditation I heard a soft whisper from my spirit guide humming in my head, "Find love and share love in the world, and you will see the divine light in everyone you meet. You will see divine light in you too. Your world will change only then."

A spiritual crisis can be a blessing in disguise. If you find yourself in such a crisis, take heart, go inside, and connect with what is most important to you. It is then that you can make conscious choices to align your life with your essence. The key is to know yourself, to love yourself, and to selflessly care for yourself. There are many good reasons not to really know and love yourself. I have heard so many really good reasons—lack of time, money, support, self-worth, self-love and not knowing what to do. The truth is that no reason is good enough!

CHAPTER 3
A Spiritual Awakening

A crisis had awoken me to the importance of aligning my life with my true essence, spirit guides, and mystical teachings. I sought out people to share my journey. There was so much to learn and remember. An adage I had heard proved true: "When the student is ready, a teacher appears." I joined a psychic development circle for serious students. The teacher was old school and very strict. She insisted that we learn to control our breath before developing our abilities. We read *The Science of Breath* by Yogi Ramacharaka,[1] which identified basic breathing techniques as the key for optimal physical health and attaining higher states of consciousness.

Weekly for three years I read Yogi Ramacharaka books as though they were the Bible. Our abilities were developed and tested in telepathy, psychometry, dowsing, mediumship, intuitive readings based on photographs and in person, seeing inside objects, and astral projection and travel.

Astral projection (or *astral travel*) is a term used in esotericism to describe a willful out-of-body experience (OBE)[2] that assumes the existence of a soul or consciousness called an astral body that is separate from the physical body and capable of traveling outside it throughout the universe.[3] This is how I observed the children who had cancer.

---

[1] Yogi Ramacharaka, *The Science of Breath* (W. & J. Mackay & CG LTD Chatham, 1903).

[2] Frederic W.H. Myers, "Astral Projection," *Journal for Spiritual & Consciousness Studies*, 37 (1; 2014): 52. Accessed October 30, 2018.

[3] John L. Crow, "Taming the Astral Body: The Theosophical Society's Ongoing Problem of Emotion and Control," *Journal of the American Academy of Religion,* 80 (3; 2012): 691–717, Accessed October 30, 2018.

Astral travel was easy for me during meditation. I could join the beings of light in bliss, peace, and calm. It is during these times I would receive guidance. I was an anomaly to the other students, who would wonder where I was and how they could go too.

Some of the members of the development circle were Reiki practitioners, and I began studying with them. The first time I placed my hands on the abdomen of my teacher, I was transported, as in astral projection, to Alaska (physically I was in Massachusetts). Overwhelmed, I appeared to be crying, but I was not crying. I felt no emotion as water filled my eyes and dripped from my nose. A friend told me the tears were a sign I was entering the angelic realm.

My hands were held fast to her abdomen as though I was under a spell. The energy flow through me was strong and unfamiliar. Although I was surprised that I could see her son and hear his thoughts, it did not stop me. I described what he was wearing, doing, and thinking. She was skeptical until two days later, when he called and relayed to her exactly what I had told her. This affirmation gave me the confidence to trust my experience and to develop my skills.

I was comfortable with the women in the Reiki circle, but I was apprehensive to tell colleagues, neighbors, and family about my work. I was apprehensive to come out and tell people that I communicate with dead people and perform astral travel. As a professional nurse, I did not want to be seen as wacky woo woo!

At times when I did tell people about my abilities, I would be marginalized or trivialized or made a spectacle for others' amusement: "Is anyone (meaning spirits) here? What do your guides say? I thought you knew everything?" Being cautious and secretive, I maneuvered around the topic to see where people stood. Determining whether they believed in life after death was a good place to start. My work was sacred to me, and I wanted it to be respected. I prayed and studied while mystical experiences continued to come to me.

In the early 2000s, I attended a Caroline Myss presentation in Boston. She ended her talk with a prayer that shifted me into a deep meditative state. I felt inspired, energized, and peaceful all at the same time. Her words, voice, and energy struck a well-known chord in me. I meditated for the next several days on her teachings. On the third day, I was awakened by my husband, David, asking me if I was okay.

He said, "You let out a horrific scream at the top of your lungs, and then you floated at least four inches above the mattress. I could place my hand between you and the bed. Then your whole body was shaking violently, like you were having a seizure. I could not wake you up. You passed out cold although you were already asleep. You looked different." I was not surprised that I did not look like myself. I felt that his observation supported the fact that something mystical had just happened.

"Where were you?" he asked, knowing that I astral travel at night. He was glad I was okay and hoped I would not have any more disruptive nights. I could not describe where I had been because it was not a place; it was an experience. It just was. I was in another dimension without time or space, a blissful state. A transmission of light was imprinted in me that would take time to fully understand. I was confused and excited. *What just happened? Could it happen again?* I prayed, "Holy Spirit, hover over me and keep me in your light."

The more I opened to other dimensions, the more experiences I had. One night in a dream-like state, I observed myself as a young indigenous woman. I had a sense that it was a previous life. The tribal healer asked me to fan a fire at the top of a mountain to signal deceased souls to transition into the light. Vigorously fanning the fire, I was so proud that I had been asked. Then I heard a man screaming, "What are you doing?" Abruptly I returned to the present time and found I was literally hitting my husband over the head with a pillow. When I explained I was fanning a fire in another time and place, he shook his head and went back to sleep.

He loosely tolerated my abilities but did not believe I could access other dimensions. Despite witnessing my levitation and seizure, David did not know what to make of my stories. He would patiently listen, acknowledge that he heard me, yet never encourage me by asking questions or requesting more details. I was disappointed that he did not share my enthusiasm.

My path has been full of such wonderful people who enriched my life while I was learning to bridge the gap between reality and the nonphysical world. Everyone I meet is a teacher. I want to share with you some of my stories so that you can get a sense of my journey. As you open to expand your awareness of that which you cannot see, you may learn to trust your instincts more. The presence of departed souls can occur in the day and night, anytime, anywhere, and anyplace. So be open to the possibilities.

***

A Woman at the Grocery Store

One day a deceased older woman walked with me as I entered a grocery store, and I acknowledged her and said, "Hello." She was silent until we approached the deli. She said, "That is my husband at the counter. This is his first time ordering at the deli. He does not know what to say. I always did the shopping. Can you help him?" So I observed his hesitancy and offered some suggestions from his wife regarding the meat and cheese selections, thicknesses, and amounts to order. He was appreciative, saying, "My wife always did the shopping." His wife asked if I would follow him down the aisles to see if he needed to find anything else. Of course, I did. I told him, "Your wife would be so proud of you. I am sure she is here with you in spirit." He nodded as he said that he felt her presence, and tears filled his eyes as he beamed with delight.

A Woman at the Local Herbarium

At a local herbarium I was at the register with a line behind me as a spirit popped in and insisted that I tell the man behind the counter that she was there. I told her that he looked very busy and this may not be good time with so many people around. She urged me to try. Tentatively I asked him if he knew a woman who had died recently and let him know that she wanted to communicate with him. He said, "Yes, my sister." She told him, "Stop being such a big baby. I am fine. I like where I am, and you knew I was going to die. Get on with your life." She instructed me to walk around the counter and give him a real hug, just like a bear. Tears filled his eyes as I shared the message; he was appreciative. He knew his sister was okay because she always gave big bear hugs.

A Husband at the Breast Cancer Center

The following story may seem sad at first, but true love is always beautiful. I attended a class at the breast cancer center with my friend,

Mary Ann, who had leukemia. She wanted to learn how to apply makeup after losing her eyelashes, eyebrows, and hair and to wrap beautiful scarfs around her head. I never knew there were so many ways a scarf could be twisted and folded. My friend has an amazing spirit and loves seeing the beauty in the world. She is a hairdresser and wrote articles in the local paper on beauty secrets. "A woman is always beautiful," was her motto.

During the class a deceased man asked me to speak to his wife. When I said hello to her, she said, "I have breast cancer for the second time." The deceased man said, "She is going to die. I want her to know I am here and that I am okay. I will be waiting for her. She will like it here. I died suddenly after a heart attack, and I never got to say good-bye. I miss her." I resisted this task, thinking, *Why me? How do I begin a conversation with a total stranger about dying?*

As I started to walk away, the love this man had for his wife filled my heart. I got out of my head and allowed the beings of light to guide me. Cautiously, with all the love in my heart, I gave her the message. I described her husband and his death to her. "Your husband is here with me and he says, 'I died suddenly of a heart attack and did not get to say good-bye. My wife was the love of my life and still is. I miss her. Although I am always with her, I just cannot hug her now.'" She nodded her head and knew the message came from him.

She smiled, saying, "I miss him too." She nodded at the news that he was always there. She said, "I feel him sometimes. I just was not sure it was him. Now that I know he is near, I feel more peaceful. I feel the cancer is going to be too much this time." She thanked me as she solemnly entered the elevator. I never saw her again, as happens with me all the time. I deliver messages, plant seeds, and move on.

***

There are so many stories I could relate to you. I hope these bring you an understanding about my process of awakening. I was convinced that something was happening between the physical reality and an invisible world. I wondered, *What is coming next? How should I serve, and what is my potential? Could I be a bridge or translator between these two worlds?* I trusted that all would be revealed to me if I continued to develop my spirituality.

Spiritualty to me is an understanding of my spirit and the universal truths gained through reflection, prayer, and meditation. The more I learned, the more I realized we cannot really define our true potential because *our potentials are limitless.* The universe holds infinite possibilities. I decided to go with the flow and trust.

Milestones and markers indicated my journey was moving in the right direction. Meditation, astral travel, dreams, and communicating with deceased souls and multidimensional beings led to my acceptance that there is so much more that we cannot see. Universal consciousness in beyond our physical reality and is a space where the impossible becomes possible. Life events, thoughts, and beliefs can cloud the truth that our light is eternal and infinite, and peace always exists within us.

There are many paths to awakening. Trauma, illness, tragedy, and near-death experiences can shake you awake to the truth that there is more than you can see and understand. Why these events happen in our lives is a mystery that we may never understand.

During our last boating season, my husband had many ocular migraines (transient ischemic attacks?) and heart palpitations that caused him to turn white and become short of breath. Western medicine investigated, and all brain and cardiac tests came back normal and said he had nothing about which to be concerned. On the contrary, I was having visions that said otherwise.

For over a year, I had several visions of David awakening at night clutching his chest and gasping for a breath, white, pale, and clammy. It looked to me as if he was having a heart attack. He did not believe in my abilities and would say things like, "That is your world, not mine. It is okay for you to believe what you want to believe. I just do not believe you can talk to ghosts." He said that dead is dead and that we do not have more than one life, let alone become ghosts after death. So I wondered, *What should I tell him? Would he believe me? Could I intervene and prevent the event? Is it all in my head?* I was not sure what to do with these visions in my dreams that seemed as real as watching a movie.

A mentor told me to "shoot him the juice," meaning to send David a laser stream of healing light and love. During the summer and fall I sent the light frequently. I also suggested he stop eating so much red meat and do more cardio. I did not tell him about my visions.

Meanwhile, I replayed the event in my head. What would I do? Call

9-1-1, CPR, pray. Did the vision mean David would have a heart attack or die? Either way, I would do all I could to support his journey with light and love. I questioned my guides, "Why am I seeing this?" The answer came, "So that you can prepare."

The night did come. David awoke clutching his chest, gasping for air, pale, and sobbing until he froze. Did his heart stop? His body appeared sucked in with his skin stretched over his bones. His eyes were wide open with fright. I sensed that he was not in his body. I kept my hand on his heart, fed him the juice (energy), and cried myself. He had a gaunt look, was white as a sheet and stiff as a board, and held his hands in a tightly flexed position as though holding on for dear life. I tried to open his hands to release some of his panicked energy. He fought me, pulling his hands away when I tried to hold them. Finally, after a deep breath in and out, he exclaimed, "Am I dying? I don't want to die."

After a full breath, he described going through a tunnel. There was an absence of sound, objects, people, or light. Once through the tunnel, he saw a park bench in a beautiful, peaceful garden. He was confused and did not know what to do, so he sat down. A woman came along and asked him why he was just sitting there. David said, "I am waiting for Kathi." In a soft, kind voice, she said, "She is not coming." Frightened, he immediately returned to his body. I had only seen David cry one time before, when his father died. On this night, he cried for hours.

When he became calm, he told me that he had seen our unborn daughter, and he cried. He said that his life passed before him, leaving him feeling empty and wrung out.

At that moment his deceased mother, Teola, appeared, her head as big as the room. She let out a haunting laugh and then disappeared after delivering a grim message: "David won't be here much longer." Teola was angry at David and me for leaving her in Texas and taking her grandchildren to New England. She called me a witch at David's father's funeral and did not want a relationship with me. Why she had appeared at this moment was puzzling to me, and why was she still angry?

My spirit guides told me that David would be okay. He went to a cardiologist and was diagnosed with Wolfe-Parkinson White Syndrome. An interventional cardiologist performed a nine-hour ablation to normalize his heart rhythm as I confidently and calmly read a book. The staff would check in on me and let me know it was taking longer than expected. I was not worried. After the procedure, the cardiologist said, "He is cured." The word *cured* seemed odd to me because the truth was his life would take on a new direction.

An old girlfriend from high school, Melissa, appeared in one of his dreams, and he thought it was strange. She had died several years earlier, and he had not spoken to her in decades. He had not been happy about how they had broken up. He had said something that hurt her. Then one morning David wanted to show me something in his closet and said, "Look, a T-shirt from my high school folded neatly on top of my clothes. I have not seen that shirt in ten years. Did Melissa put it there?" Now, not only was he seeing ghosts, he was observing metaphysical events. His experience convinced him there is an afterlife. Oh my, the change was dramatic! I was thrilled that I could share my experiences with him and that I would be able to grow as well through our conversations.

No longer the skeptic, David wanted to learn everything. I accompanied him on his journey, and it was fun and interesting. He lost thirty pounds, ate nutritious foods, went to yoga, and worked out three days a week. He became acquainted with his own guides. He told me he asked them, "Could I ever be at Kathi's level?" and he was reassured that there are no levels of spirituality. We are all on our own journeys and cannot compare ourselves.

Now he had a different view of my abilities and the possibility of an afterlife. He started having visions and dreams of his mother haunting him with messages to break us apart, and his deceased high school girlfriend, Melissa, befriended him in spirit. Melissa said, "David, you are just like you always were." Teola, David's mother, said, "Kathi will meet another man who will share her spiritual life and astral travel." She warned him that after my mother's birthday in March, he would not be around much longer. She became the grim reaper of death, as this was the second warning.

I sent thoughts of love and light to Teola so that she could find peace in the afterlife. I felt her warnings were coming from a place of anger and not even worth the breath necessary to speak them. But David seemed to play it over and over in his mind: what if it was true that I would meet someone? Of course, I said, "No way, baby. You are the only one for me."

David started referring friends to me for sessions and became a believer in the afterlife. He continued trying to understand his purpose in life. He told me he felt empty and was trying to fill himself up. He meditated, read Neville Goddard and dream books, and attended intuitive development classes. He was all in as a seeker on his own personal journey. This was the happiest I had been in our relationship; we became so close sharing our experiences. I felt blessed.

As you can see from all I have written, my awakening came after a debilitating illness, and my husband's awakening came through a near-death experience. Both of these events led to an understanding of the continuation of consciousness and the afterlife.

Physical illness, near-death experiences, loss, trauma, and devastating life events can lead to an awakening, and you cannot ever go back to the way you saw the world before the life-changing event. You are forever changed in a way that you cannot even describe. You just know you see the world, your life, work, family, and friends through a new lens. This new lens led to an initiation to learn about the invisible world that we cannot see and the inner world that we always knew was there as well as a desire to live a full, meaningful life, knowing that life is temporary and not just to be endured but enjoyed.

An initiation into the invisible world of magic and possibilities requires that you know who you are, trust you are more than enough, know that you have the power to choose wisely, and most of all have faith in the universe beyond what you can see. The following story illustrates these points.

Faith is the key to survive any storm, life experience, or transition. Faith held me steady in strong winds and forceful seas miles from shore. One day, when I was on a boat three hours from port, a storm blew in. It was worse than predicted. Violent storms rising at sea can ignite fear at the core of my being. In the critical moment when the boat lists and the waves spill over the gunnels, washing the cockpit clean, I tremble. Surrendering to the wind and waves, bobbing up and down between the swells, and struggling to stay on course had my full attention. Believe me, I was certainly living in the moment.

Not only was I terrified for myself, but my precious granddaughters were on board. We named our boat *Emma-Mia* for the two girls. *Emma-Mia* was certainly challenged as she rocked back and forth with what seemed like little advancement toward home at the mercy of the storm. Let me just say I was the only one on board who was terrified and praying.

The girls would laugh and howl at the wind and shriek with laughter when a wave came over the side and soaked them. They had no fear, so I focused on remaining calm on the outside. Of course, I knew all the bad things that could happen. I was responsible for these beautiful girls. They reminded me to relax and embrace the moment, calming me enough to react more purposefully. Papa captained the boat. A memory was being created.

Our rain gear did little to protect against the swirling wind and rain. We were soaked, cold, and tired. Taking my turn at the wheel under the guidance of my husband, he strongly suggested, "You have to be able to handle the boat in any weather just in case, right?"

"In case of what?" I asked.

"In case I get hit in the head with the boom or knocked overboard," he answered. It took all my strength to grip the wheel and hold her steady, guiding her up one swell and down the other.

Through the pellets of rain and the splashing of seawater, we lost sight of the lighthouse, our view of land that was guiding us home. Grateful for our instruments, we knew where we were and where we wanted to go even though we could not see our destination. We tacked back and forth to make headway. Cursing the sea would not get us home. We chose to embrace our journey. We set a course in harmony with the tide and current to help us along against the wind and waves.

At last we reached our homeport and disembarked the vessel. The swell of gratitude rising in my being is beyond words. "We are safe! We are on land!" I exclaimed. I drew in a deep breath and released a heavy sign. Had I forgotten to breathe? Was I holding my breath?

Since that time, many storms have come and gone, no two the same. I have survived them all. All was not lost as I am still here. *Emma-Mia*, our thirty-foot sailboat, is solid and has held tight in all weather. She always did. I learned to trust her and the sea. Riding the waves would become fun overtime, a challenge, and practice in the art of maneuvering. I learned to amuse myself by merging, molding, and melting into the flow of the sea, embracing the wind on my face.

There have been storms in my life where I have screamed out for mercy, for help, for release of the pain, for making things different or better. I pleaded for an understanding, for a reason for the chaos, for knowledge of why events had gone wrong and caused suffering. One moment I would exclaim there is no God. The next moment, I would ask why God was punishing me—irrational rationalizing. Faith helped me to keep my head and to not despair no matter what happened.

Intellectually, we all know when a storm hits that the sun still exists above the clouds. The sun will come out again and the seas will calm, but the mind may not quiet long enough for that remembering. Faith is my anchor. A leap of faith requires that you trust your anchor to hold, to accept where you are, and to trust your tools to get you to where you want to be even when you can no longer see your destination. Trust is your inner guidance system. Have faith.

A leap of faith is evidence of the knowledge that you are enough, will always be enough, and are supported by forces beyond your imagination. Learn to catch the wind and to make things happen. Faith is not an abstract mental construct; it is a deep knowing in the center of your being that all is well.

My awakening provided me with a road map through chaos, disappointment, and despair that was found through an understanding of my unique essence of light and the intimate connection between the impersonal laws of the universe, the nature of Mother Earth, and my physical body—and most important, an understanding of the consequences of holding onto fear, anxiety, and illusions.

I shared my story with you so that you may give yourself some time to reflect on the events, people, places and things in your life. Your life has been shaped by every experience in childhood and adulthood. You are a sum total of it all—the good, the bad, and the ugly.

CHAPTER 4
You Are Intuitive

You are divine light, and you come from a divine, loving universe. From birth you are blessed as an intuitive being of light with wisdom that cannot be learned or unlearned. What if you had a reliable tool that was always available, accurate, and aligned with your highest good that could tell you what to do next? Have you ever had an epiphany and thought, *Wow! Suddenly I see*? You knew the answer was there all along. The most powerful tool you have to manifest your dreams is your intuition.

In this fast-paced world, we need to trust our intuition. There is not enough time to study and evaluate every decision with the rate of change and depth of information to comb through and consider. There is so much information; it is a time of extremes in our world, a unique time in history, a rare, precious opportunity to reevaluate our lives and move forward in healthy ways.

How do you use your intuition to guide you on your life's path? Do you listen to your inner voice? When have you connected to your intuition? What has happened when you have listened to it? What has happened when you have ignored it? If you have never before considered this, it is not too late to start!

What Is Intuition?

Our intuition accesses inner wisdom that is always available to us, even when we forget. When you ignore or refuse to listen to your intuition, you can become afraid, lost, and confused and then suffer. The wisdom from every experience you ever had is permanently infused in you. When you are open and trust your intuition, you discover how intensely beautiful and useful self-trust can be. Who or what in this world unequivocally supports your best interests with every heartbeat more than *you*?

We all have it, just as we have the five senses of sight, hearing, taste, touch, and smell. We might agree that an individual who has honed his or her ability to recognize musical notes has a more developed sense of hearing. A connoisseur of fine wine or food may be able to detect subtle ingredients through a well-developed sense of taste.

You can develop your intuition by observing your mind, thoughts, words, actions, and visceral reactions in the present moment to learn when your intuition is activated or not. You need to feed and water a plant to grow, so too your intuition needs to be fed, nurtured, and developed to blossom and bear fruit. It takes practice, and I will give you tips later in this chapter.

Intuition is your inner voice, your essence, and the divine *you*—the *you* that chose to come into this world from the divine, loving universe. When you learn to trust your intuition as you trust your heart and soul, your life will flow more easily.

According to the HeartMath Institute, the heart can learn, remember, feel, and send messages to the brain.[4] What you know to be true in your heart is invariably true. Trust your inner wisdom and yourself more than anyone else, even when you cannot see the beautiful truth hidden in the moment. Your inner wisdom will always guide you in the direction you need to travel. When you follow your personal truths, you flow more easily with life.

Why Do You Have Intuition?

Intuition plays an essential role for decision-making in our rapidly changing environments. Science is only hundreds of years old, and yet our logical minds often seek measurement and proof, bypassing our intuition. The use of electronic devices to search for information and communicate with one another bypasses the traditional sharing of information from person to person. Our world is changing, and information is available at a

---

[4] "Scientific Foundation of the HeartMath System," HeartMath Institute, retrieved from https://www.heartmath.org/science/

rapid speed, much faster than our minds can discern. The ability to ignite and trust your intuition is key to survival in the fast-paced digital world. It is time to have faith in ourselves, our intuition, and one another.

An article in the New York *Times* in February 2019 described that a yearning for a science-religion synergy is growing in some circles. An example is the Formation Project, an initiative designed by a group of millennials who are looking to cultivate their inner lives and form a community by combining ideas from psychology and neuroscience with practices from ancient spiritual traditions.[5]

How Does Intuition Work?

Our bodies are constantly sensing the vibrations around us, whether we are aware of it or not. When you become curious and observe your surroundings, you can receive clues that alert you to danger and guide you on your path. Curiosity is the dance of the soul! Be curious about your life.

Gut instincts can alert you to something in your physical world. The intestinal tract has 100,000 sensory neurons[6] and the heart 40,000 sensory neurons,[7] which are cells similar to brain cells. This neural network is capable of sensing your environment to alert you. For example, have you ever gotten a feeling in the pit of your stomach that a business deal or relationship is not going to work?

This sixth sense, a soft quiet voice, is just there. Sometimes thoughts can come to mind, such as, "I know this job is not right for me," or "It is time to move or start a family." These can be examples of intuition.

What do you do with this information? Do you decide you need proof, thus discounting your inner voice? Your intuition is your inner sense of knowing. Self-empowerment comes from trusting yourself and

[5] David DeSteno, "What Science Can Learn from Religion," New York *Times*, February 1, 2019, retrieved from https://www.nytimes.com/2019/02/01/opinion/sunday/science-religion.html

[6] Adam Hadhazy, "Think Twice: How the Gut's "Second Brain" Influences Mood and Well-being," *Scientific American*, February 12, 2010, retrieved from https://www.scientificamerican.com/article/gut-second-brain/

[7] "Science of the Heart: Vol 1 (1993-2001): Exploring the Role of the Heart in Human Performance," HeartMath Institute, retrieved from https://www.heartmath.org/resources/downloads/science-of-the-heart/?submenuheader=3

your senses. What is right for one person may not be right for another. It is about being you and finding what is right for you.

It is knowing who *you* are and responding to your inner guidance system. It does not mean that you need to make a drastic change in your life immediately. More likely you may need to consider something that you are avoiding. Persistent or intense intuitive hits should be considered as important. Allow yourself time to settle in with the new information and notice the thoughts and emotions that come up in you. Maybe just write it down to get the idea on paper as a first step. If nothing else, accept your intuition as true and just sit with it. You do not need to immediately turn it over to the command center in your brain to figure out all the possible ways your life is going to change.

Where and When Do You Hear Your Intuition?

Learn to identify where your intuition is always working or never working. Where do you hear your intuition? Notice the environments that are more conducive to hearing your intuition, like taking a bath or walking in the woods. Intuition is always there and always available, just like your other five senses.

Have you ever been speaking with someone only to find out they have not heard a word you said? Maybe they did not want to hear what you were saying, or their own thoughts were dominating their mind. If you do not want to hear your intuition telling you that you need to go to yoga or the gym, you will turn it off. You can turn your hearing off, and you can turn it on. It is the same with your intuition. It requires conscious awareness and practice.

Barriers to Intuition

Many times, you avoid the truth and ignore your intuition because it may require you to make changes in your life that you view as disruptive. What if you got a sense that you need to change jobs and had no idea what else to do? You have bills to pay. What next? It is hard to hear your intuition when you have a lot of noise going on in your head.

What if every time you get an intuitive hit, you second-guess yourself and process the information through your mind? For the really big questions such as, "What is my soul's purpose?" your mind is limited to the information that you have stored from your life, knowledge, lessons, and experiences. It may be difficult to accept the limitations of your mind. The mind may say, *I cannot believe that could be true*, and then you minimize the importance of a message, even when it is repetitive.

Write down the message, thought, or word when you receive an intuitive hit, and be curious without judgment. See if you can explore how and why it is showing up at this moment in your life. Do you wonder why this inner voice is persistent and unrelenting? Your inner self wants you in this physical incarnation to connect with your authentic self for your highest possibilities and best good. An authentic lifestyle is the foundation for helping others too.

Who Are You as an Intuitive Being?

Everyone is born with a sixth sense, and to develop this sense takes patience, perseverance, commitment, kindness toward self, teachers, and a community. There are countless individuals who tell me things they have never told anyone. Their fear of being called a liar, a dreamer, a wacky woo, or even a witch has stopped them from sharing. They kept this wonderful part of themselves secret, so they did not explore and integrate it into their lives. In order for you to express your true gifts in the world be brave and listen to your inner voice.

Your intuition is a sensation that you interpret. It is not tangible. The more you practice, the more aware you become and the more you can trust it. Strong emotions and repetitive thoughts create clouds in your energy body. These clouds make hearing your intuition like trying to hear someone when the radio is blasting. You cannot hear through the noise. So quieting your mental thinking and emotions can provide clarity. More on this later in the book.

Your experience is unique to you and meant to be interpreted ultimately by you, not someone else. Our friends and family can offer insight, but it is up to you to decide your own truths. One of the keys to improving your intuition is to trust your thoughts while keeping an open mind. As you evolve, your intuition will be more specific. The universe is not static.

Energy flows and never stops moving and transforming our existence. Your growth and flexibility are keys to a long life, and intuition is your internal guide.

The following are tools to heighten your intuition. A daily or at least a regular practice will bring you amazing gifts of knowing, confidence, and empowerment to live your life to its fullest.

Quiet the mind. Mindfulness practices can bring your conscious awareness into the moment. When you meditate and silence your busy mind, you allow subconscious thoughts to emerge. When distracting, repetitive thoughts continue to loop in your head, you can send them out on a puffy white cloud. Mindful activities can help you filter out mental chatter that interferes with intuition.

Be a witness to people, places, and events and avoid the impulse to react with emotion. Strong emotions, particularly negative ones, can cloud intuition. Observe your emotions and consciously become neutral to your response to the events, the people, the places, and the things in your life. Yes, be positive! You can consciously replace the emotion with a memory of a joyful event or express gratitude to neutralize the negative emotions. Refocus and be in control!

Create a sacred space. A comfortable, tranquil place in your home can stimulate the creative side of your brain and ignite your soft, quiet voice. You can always create a safe, peaceful place in your mind to retreat, such as a memory at the beach or in the forest or garden. You can create your sacred space in your mind or in reality. A sacred space in your home, for example, could be a special chair in a comfortable room with artwork, candles, soft lighting, and pictures of loved ones.

Clear out clutter. Clutter can be physically distracting in your surroundings and in your thoughts as well. Your mind uses precious energy to remember where you put something, and that waste of energy can interfere with your ability to be peaceful and calm. You can choose to repurpose possessions that you no longer want to a good cause, and keep only what you love, need, and use. It feels good to give to others too!

Take time for solitude. Silence is a key that gives rise to compassion, creativity, and peace. Allow your mind to spend time daydreaming and imagining. Pay attention to that which comes from your subconscious. You might find a lot of information in subtle messages.

Listen to your body's signals. "Gut feelings" are a physical sensation in the body alerting you to something, trying to get your attention. Notice your thoughts or activities at the time to become more aware of something you may not have previously noticed.

Slow down your pace. Observe your present state of mind, thoughts, words, and actions. Tune into your environment and notice what you find. Few things stifle intuition as easily as constant busyness, multitasking, and connectivity to digital devices, stress, and burnout.

Go outside to be in nature. Get some fresh air and connect with nature to relieve stress and gain new creative ideas. Nature heals the spirit by calming emotions and clearing the mind.

Awaken your spiritual sight. Hold the intention of only seeing love in the world and consciously filter out all that is not love so you can clearly see and feel love and peace in your heart.

Be conscious. Observe events, people, places, and things, and keep a journal of anything that strikes you. Notice the colors, shapes, synchronicities, objects, animals, and more. Pay attention to your own experiences in a nonjudgmental way to allow your intuition to provide clarity.

Trust your messages and your wisdom. Your inner wisdom will always guide you in the direction you need to travel. Accept that what you see is what you see. Do not attach and engage the mind to perseverate on each intuitive hit; allow a flow of information and see where it leads you. Let go of the inner critic, needing to be right or more intuitive than another. Fear of being wrong or better limits the flow of energy. Go with your first choice at a restaurant. If when you glance in your closet you want to wear red, go with it. You do not need to rationalize why. Become conscious this week of your first instincts.

Allow time for imagination. Individuals who are intuitive often rely on their imagination, ideas, and possibilities. They may dream more, fantasize, and question why things happen the way they do. And they may say they always feel slightly detached from the actual, concrete world.

People who tend to be logical, analytical thinkers can block their intuition because they rely on running all their decisions through the brain. If the information does not come from logic, they often dismiss it.

Your intellect and logical mind can be distracting and misleading. If this is you, then pausing to check in with your thoughts and allowing them to rest while you access your intuition consciously will help.

Dreams

It is very helpful to write down your dreams or how you felt as you left the dream state. Your subconscious comes through in your dreams. Train your mind to remember by repeating to yourself during the day, "When I dream tonight, I will know I am dreaming."

Natural Coincidences

Animals, butterflies, birds, and more can spark our consciousness to pay attention to our own inner voice. Pay attention for recurring events in your life for messages.

In learning to use your intuition, the first thing to determine is whether you are intuitive some of the time, most of the time, or rarely. Notice where and when your intuition seems to always flow or never flow.

You can do this. We are all intuitive; it just takes practice. You may be surprised about what you discover about you and your world.

***

The following stories are examples of how to trust and explore your intuition and to be open to signs around you in your everyday life to ignite your intuition.

My Story of a Deer Sighting

Events, people, places, and things can trigger your intuition. Indigenous people believe animals carry messages for us and can come across our paths to deliver a message. The messages are to alert you to something that you may be avoiding, as in my story. Sometimes they are persistent.

I was not accepting the truth of what was happening in my marriage. My husband had formed an intense emotional relationship with another woman. I chose to live apart from my husband while we sorted out our potential future or divorce. I felt trapped in the bowels of anger, disappointment, fear of being single, and wanting to be free at the same time. I was terrified at the significant disruption in my marriage, home, career, and finances and what appeared to loom ahead. I was stuck.

Meditation was delicious and soothing. I breathed in love for myself and my husband and prayed for peace between us. My mantra was, "Whatever comes, whether we are together or apart, may I be strong and stand in my power of love." And then a word or event could trigger the anger. I could not escape.

Then, within a week, a series of four deer ran in front of my car, literally within fifty feet. Four deer are not random, as I travel these roads frequently and have rarely seen a deer. After the third deer, I became curious what the meaning could be. After the fourth sighting I knew the deer were trying to send me a message I could not ignore.

Maybe the most effective way to summarize a lesson from deer interpreted by indigenous people and the Celts is to say that "only when we move through life in the spirit of love for all beings can we melt the barriers that separate us from others and from the beautiful mystery which is our own magical and spiritual gift." [8]

My spiritual path of love for all was being tested. I was angry at myself for being angry and not being able to express my words with kindness from a loving heart. Every word I rehearsed as I tried to predict his retort fell hopelessly to the ground.

I asked the loving energy of the deer to help me release the anger. *Let it all go, please. I cannot hold any more or I will explode. Help me to open my heart to love myself and David unconditionally, to find peace and balance together or apart.*

Deer are sacred carriers of peace and teach us to be gentle, to touch the hearts and minds of wounded beings who are in our lives. Deer asks us not to push people to change, rather to gently nudge them in the right

---

[8] Ina Woolcott, "Deer Power Animal Symbol of Gentleness Unconditional Love and Kindness," February 8, 2015, retrieved from http://www.shamanicjourney.com/deer-power-animal-symbol-of-gentleness-unconditional-love-and-kindness

direction with the love that comes from deer. Love and accept people as they are. The balance of true power lays in love and compassion. [9]

The blessing and message from the four deer is that when a deer enters my world, I should be curious about a new innocence and freshness about to be awakened in me. I encourage you to be open to new adventures and the opportunity to express the gentle love that will open new doors for you. All is not lost, dear one (deer one). I thanked the deer for their kindness and love.

Fearful of Her Visions

As a child, a woman had visions that came true. She was told not to talk about spirits and visions, so she locked this part of her away. As an adult, she wanted to develop her intuition and began to meditate. The more she meditated, the clearer her visions became. Then one day she received a random intuitive hit—a vision of her young adult son lying face down in an alley in a city. They lived in a rural area, so it did not make sense to her.

She worried about her son and his future. She did not want to lose her only son, so she refused to acknowledge the vision. She kept trying to get it out of her head. Her thinking mind said, *Is he hurt? Will he recover? Is he dead?* The more she thought about him in the alley, the more upset she got. She stopped meditating and blocked her intuition to protect herself from the vision.

A year later, her son went to a bachelor party in the city and got really drunk. When leaving the bar through a side door, he entered an alley and fell face down. His friends got a picture to tease him with later. They were all standing around him, laughing at his clumsiness. He popped right up feeling a little dizzy and regretting all the alcohol he had consumed, and he went home to sleep it off.

The mother may have been able to see the story if she had allowed the vision to unfold without judgment and fear. She could have embraced her

---

[9] Ina Woolcott, "Deer Power Animal Symbol of Gentleness Unconditional Love and Kindness," February 8, 2015, retrieved from http://www.shamanicjourney.com/deer-power-animal-symbol-of-gentleness-unconditional-love-and-kindness

magnificent power of light and love and sent it to her son to protect him and ease his fall.

***

A common mistake when developing your psychic abilities is to attach to what you see and immediately translate the vision with your thinking mind. A vision is a vision and does not come from your logical mind. When I get a potentially disturbing vision, I become curious about what I am seeing. I want to see and sense beyond it. I know there is always more, so I am patient.

Do not create and ascribe meaning to a story that you want to hear. Let the vision be the vision and be curious. Ask your inner wisdom to let you know if everything will be all right. When you have fear, it makes it harder to see. This is what happened to the woman above.

I encourage you to be a witness and view from a place of inner stillness; allow the vision to reveal the next step, and witness creation unfolding before you. You can acknowledge your preconceptions, ideas, and beliefs, but resist the urge to change them. Do nothing. Instead, take a few breaths and connect with the joy of not needing to know the answer; hold space for the world to keep spinning. We all have free will, so the possibilities are always in flux.

Resist the impulses to attach emotions because when you remain neutral you allow more information to flow. Emotions can block what you see. Sometimes visions are meant to trigger something in us that we need to awaken. Remember, there is more that we cannot see.

Many times, visions are to prepare us for events or so that we can send light and love to keep someone safe. Ask your angels to be with whomever you saw and to keep them safe. Ask that, if there is a lesson to learn, it may be gentle. Send your light and love to surround whomever for the highest possibilities and best good.

You do not need to tell anyone about what you see; it is your experience. However, if you do have friends you trust, you may want to check in with them to see if they are receiving similar information. The tracking of your skills with others will give you more confidence. Keep moving forward— one day you will find you can trust your experience without validation from others. Learn to trust that your experience is your experience.

You Are Intuitive!

Be intuitive! It is your birthright! Your intuition can be ignited through synchronicities, animals, people, numbers, places, and things. Be alert to that which sparks a truth in you. When you start on a path to develop your intuition, it leads the way to learn more about you.

You are an intuitive being of light having an earthly experience. You can have fun as you ignite your intuition and flow more with life. It is informed, it knows everything about who you are, and it is timeless and eternal. This essence does not know all about all. It knows all about you. It knows your strengths, challenges, and desires.

Notice where and when your intuition always or never flows and build from there. Know you are a powerful multidimensional being with the ability to communicate through your intuition, dreams and imagination.

CHAPTER 5
Your Spirit Guides

Your intuition can be a bridge to your spirit guides and provide glimpses of the world beyond your physical reality. Spirit guides are beings of light from the nonphysical world. They illuminate mysteries, provide comfort, and sometimes explain why things are as they are. The invisible world of spirit guides can appear in your life to help you when you ask or really need them. I will use the term *spirit guide* to include angels and beings of light because the intangible communication they use is similar. It may be easier than you think to connect with your spirit guides.

Are you curious about this ability in you? I encourage you to have no fear when a deceased loved one or anonymous spirit comes into your life. As in life, there are good and bad spirits; some will wish you harm, and others will help you. If you meet a malevolent spirit, simply ask it to leave and fill your mind with love and light. On earth you have the power to ask spirits to leave. But chances are they are here for good, so I encourage you to relax, enjoy, and smile.

Childhood Spirits

As a young child, the dimensions beyond my physical reality were like the sunshine and the air that I breathe. They felt warm, beautiful, and available for everyone. I called this multidimensional existence the Other World.

Young children can often see spirits, fairies, and angels more easily than adults because their consciousness does not block out such sightings. The response of an adult is key to a child's understanding. I did not seek approval or validation. I accepted my experiences and kept my adventures to myself to avoid embarrassment or judgment. The Other World is sacred to me, although there were times when my ego would rebel against its guidance. I can tell you my life did not go well during those times.

Astral travel and being with the beings of light came easily to me as a child. I instantly dissolved into other dimensions. Stillness and absence of thought was easy in an existence unrecognizable to all five senses; there was no scent, breeze, temperature, or distraction in the quietude.

My senses were insufficient to collect data; therefore, the mind was ineffective. The mind became silent. The stillness and peace I found was magnetic. I could stay forever where there were no sounds, no images, no body, and no thoughts.

Messages from spirit guides are often spontaneous—*swoosh!* There they are. I just receive information. Other times in meditation or a dream-like state, I receive a sense of their presence without an exchange of words. I sense something has changed within me that would come to conscious awareness later. The messages became clear with time, patience, and practice. As a true Scorpio, I am intense in everything I do, even play. The beings of light would lighten me up too.

In the psychic development circle, I really opened up to the many realms of existence beyond our physical reality. The beings of light were kind and safe, but I wondered if there was evil or danger in these other realms. My first teacher told me, "Kathi, you are good, right? So only good spirits will come to you." I must admit I was skeptical. I was concerned that if I opened myself up to the spirit world of souls, I might be opening a Pandora's box. Too many movies and shows like *The Walking Dead, The Exorcist,* and *The Omen* in the seventies had prompted me to be cautious.

Of course, no one is all good or all bad; we all have flaws. All I will say for now is that like attracts like; the higher your frequency is, the more likely you will attract spirit guides from the same frequency. I will explain this phenomenon in a later chapter on embracing your unique essence where I explore energy laws.

The apparitions of dead people did scare me a little. For a while, I would have to take a second look to discern whether the image I was seeing was real or an apparition. How could I explore this phenomenon that interested me and stay safe? Spirit guides came to guide, protect, and teach me. They placed a protective shield around my body so I could monitor the souls before they could enter my consciousness.

A relationship with these nonphysical beings is priceless. As with all skills, it requires patience to learn. Spirit guides, angels, and beings of light are here to help us. I trust my guides.

What or Who Are Your Guides?

Spirits, angels, and beings of light are mysterious and appear from the invisible world to help and guide us? Many religions and indigenous cultures believe in angels, beings of light, or spirits. The concept is not new. Opening our awareness to the possibilities that they do exist and are here to help us can enrich our experiences, ease confusion, and help us make sense of our lives. We are never alone; we are all one in the universe, interconnected beyond the physical world that we can see.

Spirit guides are beings of light that may or may not have lived on earth. They come willingly to support us. Their messages may come through the appearance of birds or animals that cross your path, billboards, or random songs on the radio. When you believe and are open to the symbols and messages, they can offer subtle confirmation that you are heading in the right or wrong direction. Keep your ears open for a comment that someone might say. It may be just what you need to hear.

Some guides are with us for our entire lives, but the truth is that some come and go at specific times when their presence will help us the most. They actually know what we are going to ask before we do, so they are always prepared with the answers. Our guides always speak the truth and will do their best to provide us with the wisdom we need.

Spirit guides do not necessarily have names. They are vibrational beings, but to help you connect with them they may take on a name or gender or manifest as animals or nonhuman forms such as angels, pixies, or fairies. When you use a name, it intensifies the connection you have with them and makes it easier to connect. They will appear to you as calm beings and will not intentionally scare you. They are gentle and, as I said, are here to help. Just ask, and they will do their best to communicate with you in a way that you can comprehend. They are not here to tell you what to do but to empower you.

How to Receive a Message from Spirit Guides

There are many factors that affect how you receive messages from your spirit guides. You can ask yourself these questions to assess how you receive guidance: How easily do I listen to others? How do I receive direction or criticism? Do I accept guidance in general, or do I think I know best? As with hearing your own intuition, you need to be able to have an open mind.

It is simple to clear and create a space in your mind for guidance, but it is not easy. Oftentimes, our minds take over the command center in our heads, overriding our hearts. The heart speaks to us in symbols and feelings. The mind is literal; it cannot sense, feel, or know our hearts' yearnings.

The mind will search for stored information and gather it from random sources scattered throughout the files in your head. There are so many possible permutations. The mind never stops trying to figure things out: churning, burning, and getting nowhere, often trapping or congesting the flow of energy and leading to anxiety and despair. Your mind becomes clouded by your processing random, seemingly unimportant information.

The mind does not like not knowing the answer, so it imagines answers, creating fear and unlikely scenarios. The ego can get involved, defining what is right, fair, or just; causing further distress and suffering; and creating a loop of purposeless thoughts. These thoughts can lead to distressing emotions. Trust your intuition and your guides' messages to end this cycle.

Create a Space to Communicate

If you are not receptive to guidance, it is perhaps the greatest obstacle you will have to overcome if you want to communicate. It is hard to receive information if your mind is ambivalent or convinced of what it knows.

When stressed, you create a cloud of emotions and thoughts that form a barrier through which you may not hear your guides, so they may go through someone or something you know. You may receive an impulse to call someone on the phone or see repeating patterns of numbers, words, or messages that seem to randomly appear over and over. Spirit guides will keep trying. Your job is to be open to receive and allow a window for their guidance to fly in.

In a quiet, meditative space between the physical and the mystical realms, I have found a precious, delicate shift in how I feel that I can sink into, like lowering myself into the water at a lake—at first chilling and then very pleasant. A low-grade trepidation shifts into a warm sense of knowing you have been here before, a sense of safety, comfort, love, and sometimes bliss in this space beyond the physical realm. The path to finding this space can be found in meditation. Meditating does not have to be hard; it is mostly about allowing.

Your deceased loved ones, soul group, spirit guides, and angels are all available to assist you on your journey. The way to access these helpers is quite easy. First, we must believe that they exist and are here to help us. Many times, deceased loved ones will let us know they are near through pennies, dimes, feathers, playing with electricity, dreams, and more.

The ceiling fan in my sister's bedroom kept going on randomly at night after her husband died. She just knew it was her deceased husband letting her know that he was near and sensed he was okay. Trust your thoughts that come to mind when something unusual happens.

Other beings of light such as the angels need to be asked, although the asking is really no more than recognizing that they are ready, willing, and able to assist. Many unemployed angels are seeking work; we just need to ask and thank them. Once you are familiar with the process, you will be able to sense their love for you. Of course, when you really need them, they will appear, especially in near-death experiences.

For me and many of my clients, a spirit guide's presence is a familiar sense or feeling learned through repeated experiences. We learn to recognize their sense as we learn to recognize tastes of food. It is unique and familiar. In the presence of your guides you can sense the feeling of love and comfort, so you can bask in this familiar sense to receive and allow the frequency of love to soak into the cells of your body. This sense of unconditional, ever-present love can relieve anxiety, fear, and worry.

A spirit guide may not literally speak to you or offer a name, a biography, or a reason for being there. Yet a sense of peace soaks into your body just as the sun warms you. During this experience, a subtle transmission of knowledge may be imprinted in your energy body for an interpretation later.

Sometimes your own deep inner thoughts start to permeate your consciousness, connecting you to your higher self. Your higher self is your soul's deep, innate wisdom that knows who you are, what you are, what you need, and the gifts you share with the world. In essence, your higher self is you talking to you about you. You may need to allow time to integrate; do not force your mind to process all your thoughts immediately.

Multidimensional beings can communicate beyond words, thoughts, images, and sounds. Allow yourself to just be in a calm, meditative state to receive these transmissions. Find a space without distractions, like a lanai with birds and butterflies flying above a screen ceiling, perhaps with a waterfall gently bubbling in the background and a firm cushion to support your body and legs. You never know—you may get a surprise in your meditative state and levitate, unaware that the roof is not solid, and simply float past the ceiling.

The following is a list of suggestions to connect with your spirit guides. Read them, decide on one or two to start with, and explore which ones work best for you. We are all different, and our experiences with each of these will be unique. Try the ones that work best for you.

Get out into nature. Nature can be one of the most enjoyable and easy places to experience your guides. Just walk outside in the fresh air, be mindful of your breath, and consciously allow distracting thoughts to be released with each exhalation. If you cannot be in nature, create the experience in your mind, and your body will respond as though you are there. Walk your dog.

Avoid experiences that drain your energy. Substances or experiences that distract you from your natural state of being and drain your energy—such as excessive alcohol; caffeine; sugary foods; loud, chaotic environments; and people who zap your energy—should be avoided. These can be disruptive when trying to connect to your spirit guides. In order to perceive the presence of your guides, you need to have a clear channel. It is sort of like adjusting the channel on a transistor radio.

Consider walking, yoga, exercise, qigong, and tai chi. Build ease and flow into your life. Find whatever stirs something inside of you in a joyful way. Explore music, art, nature, or children playing to see the world through the lens of what brings you joy. Lightening your heart creates a space to connect with your spirit guides. Joy can create a portal for communication.

The more you quiet your mind, connect to your heart, and breathe gently and calmly, you create a space to invite your guides. When you create a space to support this precious communication with intention, it becomes effortless. Your attention to the process is important because it honors your connection in a beautiful, graceful way and removes blocks. I crave silence in meditation as I enter a multidimensional space where the meaning to life and the sparks of creativity are born and where synchronicities are deployed to earth. It is in this sacred silence where I meet my guides.

Anytime you sense an uneasy feeling associated with advice, then the guidance you're receiving may be coming from a lower vibrational source (ego). You can shrug it off and ignore it. Your emotional response to guidance is like a navigation system alerting you to bad advice, so pay attention to it. Restate your question and wait for your spirit guide to respond.

Guides are not here to flatter you or agree with you. Never say, "Should I?" because it is like asking an outside force (ego) to take over; do not surrender authority. Be open to messages, but do not edit them to fit your agenda (ego). The ego, for most people, has been running the show. To surrender the ego to the higher self takes practice. Be patient with yourself as you develop your relationship with your spirit guide and higher self.

The whole point of guidance is to open yourself to new ideas, new solutions, and ways of working things out that you did not see before. Start each day open to guidance and with a receptive heart. The more you accept guidance, the more you attract it. Trust the guidance you receive. Repeat it out loud or write it down, especially if you receive recurrent messages or experience a series of coincidences that seem related. Act on the guidance you receive. Start by acting in small ways until you get comfortable; your positive results will lead you.

Beings of light are available to guide us on our journeys, to remind us when we get off course, and to help us make conscious choices. Meditation is a process to connect to your heart and align with your guides. Find others who you can share your experiences. When you validate your experiences with others, it can lead to better and more frequent communication and build trust. Always thank them for their presence and guidance. Thank your guides!

The following are messages I received from spirit guides whose wisdom I will cherish forever. Spirits guides can just show up and offer their wisdom to us. Although some people can actually see their spirit guides, most of us simply get a sense of their presence.

Babu

A client asked me to clear spirits from his land who were mischievous and frightening to his family. During my meditation process to connect my intuition to the land, I came across a spirit guide. He called himself Babu,[10] which means "grandfather" in Swahili. The souls felt bound to the land and did not want to leave. Babu was protecting, loving, and guiding them. Babu taught me about voodoo and his cultural traditions. I learned that voodoo is a deeply spiritual practice. He wanted me to understand their beliefs so that I could better assist his people into the afterlife. His most salient message to me was as follows:

> They say we are dirty, inferior and could not come into the house unless washed and directed to do so. We were given scraps to eat after working hard all day. Our blood, sweat and tears seeped into the soil we tilled, planted, and harvested. We cared for their animals and prepared the food they ate with our hands. Our dead bodies were buried in the earth where water flowed beneath the surface. The well water became the water they drink. They do not know it—fools to think we are separate from the air that is breathed. The wind carries our breath and our spirits beyond the field we plant and toil. We are the earth, we are the air. We are free! Our spirits are free!

I was moved deeply by this transmission and was honored to bring light and love for the transition of his people into the light.

---

[10] *All Baby Names*, s.v. "Babu," accessed November 2018, retrieved from https://www.allbabynames.com/m/BabyName/African/Babu.aspx

Red Cloud

After I visited a one-thousand-year-old Pueblo village in Taos, New Mexico, I sensed a deep connection to the earth, land, and spirit of the people. When telling friends about my day, I called a member of the tribe a Native American.

In a dream that night, a dark man with long, black braids and a hardened face told me he was my father and his name was Red Cloud. Red Cloud could not contain himself. His message was harsh and clear. In a strong, deep voice commanding respect, he blasted at me: "You have forgotten who you are. I am not any kind of an American. That is a label made up by white men to put us beneath them—just a category in their language. I am Lakota. You are Lakota too."

My mother said the name Louise came in on the wind when she gave me my middle name. Louise is the name of Red Cloud's daughter.[11] My heart tells me I am connected to the Lakota in many spiritual ways. Since then, the words *Native American* get stuck in my throat. I now say *indigenous people,* and I hope that you will too.

Amen

During a deep meditation, I received a message and journaled it immediately so that I could preserve it. This is what I wrote in my journal:

> It is not up to you to heal or relieve suffering, and it should not be your intent. As an energy practitioner your goal is to clear the energy field so that individuals can reset and find their own way. Your role is to honor their soul's journey so that they can embrace life as their teacher. Once a lesson is learned you can remove energetic remnants that remain stuck in their energy field and release what no longer serves them.

---

[11] Geni, s.v. "Louise Richard," accessed November 2018, retrieved from https://www.geni.com/people/Louise-Richard/6000000058863705076

When relationships implode, jobs are lost, children leave home, or age comes into play (how much time do I have left?), they seek help, guidance, and support for their journey. You can only plant seeds, till the soil, and perhaps shed some light and offer hope. You are a guide.

Often, they are stuck on blaming others, on finding external reasons that things are the way that they are. People rarely pause to observe their own interiors. Often their overwhelming lives fill every moment and blur a connection to their interior beings. Many have no time, no skills, and no spiritual connection, which leaves them feeling lost. Your intuition will highlight areas that they can explore in themselves.

Miracles already exist. Connect your divine light to miracles and dissolve anything that leads to separation from source energy. We like even your lower self. We love all parts of your being. You need to remind everyone to love themselves, to dissolve judgment, to want something to be different, and to embrace the journeys of their children, careers, and relationships. We are all one.

Imagine you become a wave in the ocean; the wave comes and goes. It is never the same and is never still. There is always another wave with constant movement of the water. When walking on the beach, you anticipate that the water will splash your feet, then one wave comes and unexpectedly soaks your legs. You are not angry at the ocean for being the ocean. Why be angry at a human for being human? Every wave is unique. Every wave is perfect. No wave is right or wrong, better or worse—just different and is what it is in each moment in time.

Allow flow in your life to maintain a high vibration, free your mind, and get out of your own way. Trust that the

flow of life is doing what it is supposed to do. Work to
raise and maintain the highest possible vibration of light
to balance and attract abundance, peace, and calm. Ride
the wave of life and let go of the resistance to what is.

My spirit guides remind me of the ancient universal truths that are
relevant today. Universal wisdom is within all of us, and all you have to do
is expand the radiant light within you to dissolve your physical, emotional,
and mental bodies to see clearly. A revelation! Everything I have ever heard
or learned really came from inside of me.

***

The following is a story of a client who was at a crossroads between
a lucrative career and a vocation and reconnected to her spirit guides.
She came to see me to ignite a spiritual awakening because she realized
something was missing in her career and relationship. She wanted to
experience more joy and discover her true vocation.

She absolutely glowed; her spirit was open and adventuresome. In
my mind's eye, I observed the vibrancy of her spirit as she welcomed her
spirit guides. They entered my healing energy space as a soft, violet light
filled the room. I sensed that her spirit floated easily above her body as
she played and communed with her spirit guides. They seemed familiar
to her as though she had always known them. I sensed she was from the
same soul group.

A soul group is like a family with its own secrets, traditions, memories,
abilities, and characteristics. It is beyond words when a soul connects with
its soul group; it is a sense of jubilation and celebration. This remembering
sparked and awakened an essence at the core of her being.

Immediately I had a sense that the spirit guides came to comfort and
remind her of her uniqueness as a being of light. She had a sense of longing
that felt like a sadness resulting from missing her allies. As I continued
to clear her energy body,[12] she spontaneously touched her heart. She was

---

[12] The energy field of the body can become congested with psychic free radicals,
emotions, and thoughts. The field can be cleared by sending a higher frequency of
energy through my hands to disperse the lower frequencies. More on this in later
chapters.

enveloped in the violet light that illuminated her heart and soul. I sensed an integration of her human and divine self that filled her with love.

The beings of light welcomed and enjoyed being with her too. After the session, she said, "I feel exuberant, blissful, whole, perfect, and so wonderful. How can I do this on my own? I felt like I left my body, and time seemed to stand still. I wished my experience would last forever."

She was instantly optimistic and excited by the reunion and the experience of the violet light. I thought, *Wow, she is simply remembering. This will be easy.* I gave her some guidance to be open and curious about her experiences. I let her know she could ask a question before starting to connect with her spirit guides. She could ask for guidance, love, support, understanding, and acceptance of who she is. The beings of light and violet rays of light filled her not only with love but the power of love.

The experience ignited her heart's desire and reframed her career perspective. She realized her amazing potential to send her power of love into the world.

The spirit guides let her know that they were ready, willing, and able to assist her in any way she asked. She recounted, "The proof is in the miracle of my only son. I prayed for him and felt my body fill with grace before I conceived." She said, "I have the confidence to explore a vocation to bring more light to the world and help people see their potential."

She transitioned from her a lucrative career as an attorney to her vocation as a life coach over several months. She took many courses and became certified in many modalities. She digested much information from experts and leaders in the coaching field to create her own unique brand of healing, coaching, and body work. Her spirit guides offer unconditional love, guidance, and most of all support that she is on the right path.

***

It takes time to communicate with your spirit guides. You can always create a place in your mind, whether it is make-believe or real.

It is in these precious moments that you are most open to connect your own unique essence to allow communication. Find your path to communicate through what stirs your soul and makes you feel whole. Where do you feel safe, peaceful, and easy? Trust that when you set an intention for guidance, it will come in a form that will work for you.

Once you connect with your spirit guide, you can feel a sense of comfort, love, and safety. You recognize you are not separate and realize that you are connected to something more than can be seen on the earthly plane. You receive a confirmation that help is near. Many times, when a guide appears, a joyous sense of reunion emanates throughout your body, and you receive a sense of knowing they are present without a visualization of a form.

Have fun as you explore the possibilities. Your being open is the key. Spirit guides are closer than you think!

Summary of a Nonphysical Reality

Everything you have learned in life is ultimately about you—you as a child, you as an adult, how you love, how you receive love, and how you share your gifts with the world. What if everything you have ever heard, experienced, or learned came from inside of you—a place of wanting to clear karmic debt, to gain an understanding, to reach your potential, or to evolve your consciousness?

When you choose to develop intuition and connect with spirit guides, you unlock a rich resource inside of you that can provide a pathway to your higher self and your soul's purpose.

The major points from this section are as follows:

- You are a divine being of light, and you come from a divine loving universe.
- From birth you are blessed as an intuitive being of light with wisdom that cannot be learned or unlearned.
- To trust your intuition is to trust your own heart and soul. Who or what in this world unequivocally supports your best interests with every heartbeat more than *you*?
- Your intuition does not know all about all; it knows all about you.
- The invisible world of spirit guides will appear in your life to help when you ask or really need them. Remember the salient moments of your life; where were you and who was there for you? Who are your earthly teachers? Could they be your spirit guides?
- Meditation and other processes to quiet your mind and emotions can open you to hear your intuition and your spirit guides.
- Meditation does not have to be hard; it is mostly about allowing.
- You can ignite your spirit when you remember the joy and laughter in your life. The more you reflect on these precious experiences, the more you fill your heart with love.

Love your journey and love your life. It only gets better from knowing who you are!

PART 2
An Understanding of Souls between Worlds

Grief can provide an opportunity to understand who we are at our core. I will start my discussion with the loss of loved ones and then draw you into the mystical realm of the afterlife and our existence before birth so that you can embrace that you are a soul having an earthly experience.

My goal is for you to embrace your unique essence of light and to move beyond human constraints and your focus on tasks in the external world. An earthly experience is all about becoming you and fulfilling your soul's purpose. It is the foundation for living a meaningful, joyful life.

CHAPTER 6
A Journey to Understand the Mystical Realms through Grief

How you respond to grief can teach you about who you are and lead you to who you want to become. I found my understanding of a soul's journey through the lens of grief. Grief can unlock mysteries about the truth of who you are. As you know, grief is ubiquitous to any loss. We grieve the loss of relationships, jobs, homes, finances, and loved ones. The lessons we learn through grief can be the most salient. A deep pain in your heart cannot be ignored. As humans, we do not have the power to change what is. What is *is*, and that is all there is to it.

My mother died a few days before I started writing this. Grief is strongly present in my body, mind, and spirit. In her last hours on earth, she said to me, "This is so familiar, like I have done this before. Have I died before?" I miss my mother, yet I know that she made choices in her life such that her ascension into God's garden was peaceful and effortless. Hours before she died, the room filled with the unmistakable scent of flowers. My heart is wrenching among sadness, love, and celebrating the gift that she was to me. My knowledge that she is an eternal being of light comforts me. I believe she is always with me and that I can sense her eternal love for me. Although I am sad that she is no longer with me, the joy of having had her in my life is much brighter.

We cannot change the past, only our response to our situations. Grief comes in cycles, no matter the reason for the loss—whether a relationship ended, a loved one died, a career was lost, we experienced a change in lifestyle, children left home, or any event occurred that changed your life forever. Grief can remind you to love yourself more and to create more flow in your life. The cycles of grief can become less intense, less frequent, and last a shorter duration of time when you love yourself enough. The process is not linear; the waves come and go. We can never go back in time, only forward, so why resist the ebb and flow of grief?

Do not resist the days you need to cry. Simply cry, hold yourself with your own loving arms, darken the room, and incubate your spirit as though you are forming your own special cocoon. This is your cocoon in which to heal, nourish, and nurture yourself, and when you are ready, chew your way out and fly like a butterfly. Honor your process in your own way. You can retreat to your sanctuary whenever you need to lament and return to the world renewed.

When you accept that your tears cleanse your soul to clear emotions and heal, then you will see more clearly. You can embrace an inner knowing that you are a divine being of light and that grief is only a sensation in your body, although the sensation of grief is heavy and can be overwhelming.

Some days, grief comes over us like a gentle wave, comforting us with its warmth and remembering. Other days, it can feel like we are hit by a tsunami and knocked off our feet. This cycle of grief is a process that is in constant motion. What is right for you is inevitably right for you. There are many ways to grieve: you can clean your house, pray, find solitude, cry uncontrollably, conduct a celebration of life rituals, plant trees in memory of a loved one, and create public remembrances.

Grief is an electromagnetic charge in your energy body; it is moving, so you can move it out. It is a charge, and you can release grief in the energy body to downgrade from a hurricane to a tropical storm to a gentle breeze. You are a powerful being of light and can heal your body. There will be more on this in later chapters.

The weight of grief feels palpable in the body. So many times, the sense of holding the grief feels like you are holding onto that which you can no longer have in physical form. I assure you that what you are sensing is a charge in your field and not the essence of a loved one who died. The energy of a loved one will not feel heavy or sad.

Love and joy move grief out. Choose your thoughts wisely. A joyful memory of someone you lost can spark an essence of joy to move through you as though you are experiencing it now and help to heal grief.

There can be phases of grief. One of the phases has to do with moving on and embracing your life. The key is seeing grief as a phase and not to get stuck in sadness that limits your life force and affects your loved ones, career, home, and community. Pleasant memories can allow you to be happy, so keep them alive as best you can. Each day is a new day. A universal truth is that peace lies within you and is ever present; find a quiet moment to connect to your inner peace.

You may wonder, *Is there a right way to grieve? Am I doing it right? Should I have moved on? Why am I still crying at night? Will I always be alone?* These thoughts ultimately lead to suffering. Love yourself and accept that you are doing the best you can. Accept that it is a process, and trust that time heals all wounds. Seek help from professionals to help get you through if you need to. Remember to accept what *is* to heal.

The following stories are examples of messages I have received from souls. I am including them to expand your ideas about what may be true for you and someone you love who died. These stories are about letting go of the humanness of the soul that departed the earthly plane, to see them as eternal beings of light on their own journeys, and to accept that as humans we have lives to live as well. Grief limits our ability to live our lives to the fullest. The idea is to quiet your mind and trust the messages you receive from your heart. Our human minds can create what they want to believe and sometimes attach to the first idea that comes to mind. Your intuition and spirit guides can help you to be open to hear the truth.

An Overdose

A young man addicted to substances, mentally confused, and emotionally unstable was found unresponsive. He was revived and airlifted to a medical facility, where he was put on life support. His brain was seriously damaged. The night before, he had an intense argument with his brother about his risky lifestyle.

A week after he was taken off life support, his aunt, a very spiritual person, sensed he was struggling in the afterlife and contacted me. I told her that I would meditate to clear my mind and focus on him to see if I could help. I would call her back.

My preparation for all sessions is to center, ground, breathe, and connect to spirit. I close my eyes to avoid distractions in the room. I breathe slowly to clear my mind, body, and emotions to bring my full conscious attention to stillness. At this moment I have no thoughts, no emotions, no body, no time, and no space. This process takes much practice. The clearer I am, the clearer the information I receive will be. This is how I am able to interpret the energy field of a client, whether deceased or alive. I then invite in the light, love, and energy of the earth and the cosmos to fill my body with light and love. This enhances my claircognizance. Here, I ask that you trust my process and stay tuned to learn more about you how can do this too. How I do this will become clearer in the chapters on energy medicine.

I am fully present and focused on the spirit of this young man. I found his spirit swirling in the gateway, confused and struggling. He was able to tell me that he did not want to die and said, "Tell my mother I was already gone when they found me. My spirit had left my body before I was airlifted out." He added, "Tell my brother I love him and know that everything he said was true, and I should have listened to him. I do not need any more burdens (in the afterlife) with the weight of his regret. If he thinks I committed suicide or overdosed on drugs because he yelled at me, he is wrong. Everything is on me. This is my fault."

His spirit was frantically yelling, "I am so stupid! Such a stupid mistake! I am so stupid!" In turmoil, he resisted the light and continued to be agitated, literally spinning and unable to make forward movement. I called angels, beings of light, and loved ones to surround him in love and light to calm and guide him into the light. He struggled, not feeling worthy and berating himself. I felt like we had to wrestle him a bit to settle him down. After some time, he acquiesced and found refuge in the healing plane.

His family appreciated the messages from the young man and intuitively sensed his last breath would be on August (the eighth month) 18 at 8:18 p.m. in the year 2018. The time of his death occurred at that precise time. This aligned the family with his spirit and gave comfort to them. The mother worried about taking him off life support; the brother wondered if he had pushed him too far. The young man who died was able to relieve their burdens and comfort them.

The moral of the story is that, often with a tragic death or the death of a child, we are left to wonder why our loved ones could be taken from this world. This understanding may not be a blessing that we are given. Families can accept that they did the best they could with the challenges that they faced. We are not all-powerful beings. A belief in a higher power and trust that there is a bigger picture and greater good helps to heal grief. This is harder said than done, for sure. It takes time and is a process. It takes a leap of faith.

A Tethered Soul

One day while driving, I passed a cemetery, and the spirit of a young man wearing a T-shirt and blue jeans jumped into the passenger seat of my car and said, "You have to talk to my mother." I thought, *Who are you? And who is your mother?* I saw a vision in my mind's eye of a man in his early twenties, thin and agitated as though he was in a rush. I was not from town and did not know his story. The scene of a motorcycle accident appeared in my mind as though I was watching a movie. The young man said, "My mother is distraught and cannot move on with her life. It is really hurting my younger brother." He showed me a cord to his mother through which he sends love to her but said she uses the cord to anchor him to earth. He said that it was limiting his movement forward in the afterlife. His mother's grief anchored him due to the depth of her emotions. I agreed to reach out to her. I learned that she tells her story over and over and continues to receive sympathy from her neighbors and friends. It was clear that the story of her son's tragic death was too much for her to bear. The mother became a victim, no longer able to function as a loving mother or wife. The son wanted me to make her stop.

When I arrived at my destination in town, I inquired about this young man. A fund-raiser was coming up the next week, and flyers were all over town about a young man who had died in a motorcycle accident. So figuring out who he was was not hard. The mother organized a fund-raiser every year in memory of her deceased son. I learned that everywhere she went in town, she wore her grief on her sleeve, becoming emotional and crying as people would offer their condolences. After years, her grief was as fresh as the day he died.

I contacted the mother, who was skeptical. Her face was worn and tired, and her body slumped. She looked exhausted. I offered her my condolences and acknowledged how difficult the past few years must have been on her and her family. Solemnly she nodded while looking down at her feet, not really wanting to engage with me.

I relayed her son's message: "I want you to let me go, release your anger and grief, and move on with your life to enjoy your family, who need you. I love you and want you all to be happy." I continued, "He told me, 'She needs to stop. I feel her pain and grief. I cannot bear what she is doing to my brother. I need to move on, and she is sapping my life force and it just is not fair.'"

She said, "I do not believe my son is able to communicate with you or that he would say that to me. How can I be happy when my son is dead? No mother should have to lose a son."

When asked about her faith and thoughts on an afterlife, she said, "I don't believe in God. If there was a God, why would my son be dead? I do not believe in heaven." I could sense that her chest was heavy with grief. She told me, "I hate the man who killed my son. He was so careless. I am so angry." She added, "The pain in my chest is all I have left of my son."

I told her, "Grief is not the frequency of the person who died. You are not holding onto your son." I explained, "We are connected to our loved ones through a healthy, vibrant cord infused with light and love. You are sending your pain and suffering to your son along that cord." I let her know that she can summon angels, ancestors, guardians, and beings of light to heal herself and to propel him forward in the afterlife. I offered her a healing energy session or another time to talk after she had time to think about it. She declined. The son released the cord between them and moved on.

It was a careless accident, just one of those things that happens. The mother's overwhelming grief led to poor decisions regarding the health of her family. The son loved his family. He would return to send them love but no longer felt responsible for making his mother happy. My prayers go out to her as I write this several years later. My hope is that she has accepted her son's death and moved on to live her life and to support her family.

The moral of the story is that losing faith in God or a higher power is common during these really tough transitions. When you blame others, you can create anxiety that leads to poor physical and mental health as well as disrupts relationships. Our children who leave early want us to be happy and content with our lives. They do not want us to be sad and stop living our lives. It takes great strength and courage to love yourself enough to bear the pain of losing a child so that you can live your life to its fullest one day at a time, moving forward and then backward and then forward again until one day, you can find fulfillment again with a blessing from the child who died.

She Fell in the Pool and Hit Her Head

A woman in her forties came to me with a belief that her mother had committed suicide. Although she was never sure, the police said it looked like an accident. The family found an entry in her journal that read, "I do not want to live anymore. It (depression) is so hard." The woman told me, "Clinical depression runs in my family, and my mother was depressed at the time."

Chronic anxiety and depression spanned three generations of women. My client was overwhelmed with anxiety and fear. She was angry at her mother for leaving her as a teenager, she felt anxiety and fear about her own experiences with depression, and her daughter's current depression scared her to death. "What if my daughter commits suicide because it runs in the family?" she cried. "I do not want to lose my daughter. I do not know how to help her."

Whoosh—I felt a cold chill. I sensed the energy of a spirit immediately between me and my client. It was the mother's spirit that jumped between us and adamantly said, "I fell in the pool and hit my head. I was depressed, but I never would have left you."

A conversation ensued between the mother and the daughter. The mother shared loving messages about the granddaughter that brought relief and hope to the woman. The woman could feel her mother's spirit in the room and trusted the messages I shared with her. The woman could release her fear by changing her thoughts to the possibility that her mother had an accident. Her mother's words gave her confidence that her daughter would be okay.

The moral of the story is that we are souls on our own journey. We do not have to follow the history of our family. Why would you allow your mind to create a fearful scenario? Why would you think the worst? Instead, use your powerful mind to be positive and hope for the best. There is always hope, and we can put our energy into hope instead of worry.

A Widow Maker

Jane's husband died unexpectedly in his sleep from a widow maker heart attack. She shared her story through tears and sobs sitting tensely on the edge of a chair. She had gained a lot of weight, consoled herself with food, and had not left the house since he died. She was referred to me due to overwhelming stress and anxiety, not being able to clear her mind or decide what to do next.

She told me her story. "My husband owned a business that was our livelihood, and I cannot run it on my own. We have no children, and I am fifty-one years old and alone. My parents and favorite aunt died within the past three years. I attend a Christian church every Sunday but don't really believe in heaven even though that is what my church teaches. I feel abandoned by everyone who really loved me. I behaved as everyone wanted me to my whole life, pleasing others. I never had to make decisions for myself. As a child and an adult, I was always deeply loved and cared for, wanting nothing and even doted on a bit." Her voice became more excited as her words flew as though a release of deep emotion was flowing. "What do I want? Who am I? How will I survive?" Her sobbing was uncontrollable as she expressed her fears.

The woman could not stop crying or halt the defeating self-talk that kept her in deep state of inertia. She lived a self-professed blessed life, where everything had fallen in place for her since childhood. She had given up her individuality to get along, avoid confrontation, and avoid responsibility for herself. She said, "I can't even make good choices to take care of my body. Look at me—I am so fat."

As she described this truth to me, her body tensed and her breathing became shallow. I thought that she might hyperventilate. I focused her mind on her breath in this moment, telling her, "In this moment, you are fine. Just breathe." I made my breath audible so that she could more easily find her rhythm. We breathed together slowly and calmly until she could take in a full breath and exhale fully. After several minutes, she relaxed and laid down on the massage table I use for the healing energy sessions. I played soft music, dimmed the lights, and lightly covered her with a sheet.

I prepared for the session by clearing my mind, body, and spirit so that I could interpret her energy. I could sense the fine, subtle energy swirling frenetically around and within her body, creating static and discomfort. I used my hands to send calm, clear energy through her field, moving out the static. As I smoothed out the swirling energy in her field, she expressed, "I do not ever remember being this calm and peaceful. How is this possible? I feel confident in myself in a way I have not felt before."

She relaxed as I continued to hold my hands above her body to clear more of the congested energy. She recounted many visions of her deceased father, aunt, and grandmother that she saw during the healing energy session. "My father was at the lake we went to growing up. I was waterskiing. He was so patient, and it took me so long to learn. My aunt and I went shopping together on Saturdays. She was a second mother to me. Grandma came through with her unconditional love." She felt loved. Angels were present, sending her healing light and love. Tears came to her eyes as she sensed love filling her physical and spiritual body from her deceased loved ones. She proclaimed, "They are still with me!"

After the session, she admitted she had been skeptical about energy work and was amazed at her new attitude on life. She is a beautiful woman with a huge, compassionate heart for others. She agreed that she needed to find love in her heart for herself. She pulled an angel card from the Archangel Oracle Card deck[13] and asked an angel for a message. A guardian angel, Jophiel, reminded her about the beauty of nature, her beauty, and the beauty of the world.

She said that nature, birds singing, and the scent of pine always ground her to the earth. She plans to be in nature every day even if only in her mind to find the beauty in her world and reflect on the blessings in her life. She is moving on.

The moral of the story is that self-actualization is often prompted by a tragedy, a trauma, or the death of a person. The grief from her loss was as deep and as painful as the lack of love for herself and the fear for her future. The death of her husband opened the door to discover who she really is and what makes her happy. She needed to write a new story. With faith

---

[13] Doreen Virtue, *Archangel Oracle Cards* (Carlsbad, CA: Hayhouse, Inc., 2004)

in God, hope, and confidence, I suggested she tell herself, "I got this. All is well. There is no separation. Your loved ones are closer than you think. You are never alone."

***

When is enough enough? How much can you hurt before you decide it is time to let grief go? Grief is a weight in the body, especially in the chest, lungs, and heart. Clients tell me that feeling the pain of grief can seem better than the empty feeling of loss, doubt, and fear.

Grief and a sense of loss can create a dense mass in the heart energy center and can make the chest feel heavy; with time, it can even cause the heart to become rock solid, as though protecting the heart from more hurt. A solid heart cannot receive or give love. In order to penetrate this layer of protection, personal courage is required.

A belief in the afterlife can help to relieve grief. However, grief often brings with it buried emotions and unresolved grief that can be overwhelming. It requires courage to face the unknown. It can be daunting to prepare for a new life when someone is left to carry on, raise a family, manage a business, recreate who they are, and find a new relationship. A full range of emotions can come up, such as fear, loneliness, anxiety, sadness, and despair. These emotions add to the suffering and need to be addressed with love for self.

The conclusion is that grief can be your guide to that understanding because it reaches the core of who you are and what is important to you, and it can uncover emotions that rock your world. The death of a loved one can be an opportunity to journey into your soul. You can learn to fill a void created by a loss to open you to new possibilities and growth. You can explore dormant treasures within your being. It can be exciting. I have heard from many spouses who lost their partners and found wonderful treasures of strength, new friends, and adventure.

A belief that it is time for the suffering to be over and that you have learned what you need from the person, place, or thing that you lost is the first step to healing. When you acknowledge that you are complete in your suffering and state, "I choose to move on," magic happens. Your readiness to move on allows life force to flow through you again. When you build the strength to accept what is, you can become brave and courageous as you move forward one day at a time.

Tell your friends, "I am fine, and so are they. We are all moving on and embracing our lives on earth and in the afterlife. All is well."

CHAPTER 7
Souls Transition to the Afterlife

Ancient wisdom, religion, near-death experiences, and past-life regressions suggest that there is a nonphysical reality where souls will continue to learn, to heal, to guide, and to build their capacity to love the world. Movies, books, and qualified clairvoyants have led many skeptics to open their minds to the possibility of an afterlife where our spirits continue to exist after leaving the earthly plane. I want to plant this seed in your mind: if there is a spirit that lives on after death, where is that very same spirit today? Is it possible to prepare for death?

In the past decades, books and movies written about near-death experiences (NDE) have become popular, as have those about out-of-body (OBE) experiences, describing a peaceful, loving existence in a nonphysical world.

Some are convinced that NDEs have a scientific explanation. The visions could be caused by a spike in neural activity in the brain as it approaches death, for example. But many of those who have experienced NDEs aren't satisfied with a scientific explanation, saying that the spiritual nature of such moments are too numerous and widespread to discount entirely.[14]

The near-death experience may be as close as humans get to glimpsing something out of this world. It seems to happen to some people when their heart stops and they're flatlining. Once revived, they remember

---

[14] Carol Kuruvilla, "Teen Claims He Visited Heaven During Near Death Experience," *Huffington Post*, May 15, 2018, retrieved from https://www.huffingtonpost.com/entry/teen-claims-he-visited-heaven-near-death-experience_us_5afb1ffae4b044dfffb669ef, accessed September 11, 2018.

floating above their bodies. They believe they reconnected with a deceased loved one or they say they suddenly understand the meaning of life. The accounts are remarkable and widespread, transcending age, language, culture, and geography.[15] These people often do not want to return to their bodies on earth.

Ancient traditions include rituals to celebrate and prepare individuals for their transition to the afterlife. A belief in heaven in many religions offers a safe place for healing and reward for a life well lived. In Eastern religions the belief in reincarnation means you will never really die; you will live again. Some traditions burn the body to facilitate the release of the spirit into the afterlife.

Where we go and what we do, think, or feel when we die is a mystery. All we have is faith and signs. Do we go to a vacuum of nothingness or return to a beautiful, loving world from whence we came? Ancient teachings and current scientific evidence suggest that each of us is a unique essence of light and that our essence will transcend the physical world into the nonphysical world at death.

To die is a normal part of the cycle of life. What is unknown is the time and circumstances around our departure and what follows. The birth and death of a loved one is a part of the cycle of life that occurs in all of nature. To die is to be born into the afterlife, and to be born is to leave the afterlife to enter the physical world.

Each of us has experienced or will experience the death of someone close to us. Asking yourself a few questions can prepare you to heal and to support family and friends.

First of all, what do you believe about the afterlife? Have you experienced the death of someone close to you? How certain or uncertain are you about your beliefs?

I have learned much about the afterlife over the past forty years, and I know what I know from those experiences. An individual's experience with a departed soul is as unique as each individual and the current time and space he or she is in. We assign meaning to events and sensations based on where we are in the moment. The more you trust your own experiences,

---

[15] *Today*, "Do You Believe? Near-Death Experience Survivor Recalls 'Amazing' Encounter," December 19, 2016, retrieved from https://www.today.com/health/near-death-experience-survivor-recalls-amazing-encounter-t105964

the more you will shape your own ideas. There is always more to know. I do not know the solid answers regarding what the afterlife is, specifically. My experiences give me a sense of what might be true.

Whatever beliefs you have now, I ask that you keep an open mind as I share the experiences I have had with souls who have departed. This much I know is true. Take it, sift it, and with gentleness and kindness keep what is worth keeping and blow the rest away. A gut instinct or intuitive hit that resonates as true for you is invariably true for you as it comes from your higher self.

The physical body dies with the last breath, and the spirit lives on in eternity. There is no heaven, hell, or purgatory. We are admitted to the afterlife no matter our race, our culture, our socioeconomic status, or our beliefs. It is open for all, even those who make egregious decisions while in their physical bodies.

As an individual prepares to leave the earthly plane, their deceased family members, angels, and guides show up to let them know they are near and will guide them into the mystical realms of the afterlife. Many times, individuals have dreams of loved ones prior to their death. Or in their last days, they tell family members, "Uncle Joe was just here" even though Uncle Joe has been dead for a decade.

Your loved ones will come prior to death to remind you about the afterlife so you can be alert during your transition and settle in more smoothly. They want you to trust and know you are loved, supported, and not alone.

Some souls hover over the death place, pausing to say good-bye before entering a tunnel or crossing a river or a bridge, which function as a gateway to the afterlife. Picture in your mind that you are standing at the bank of a river. Your family and friends are shouting, "Don't go! Don't go! We will miss you!" Your soul family is on the other side welcoming you home and celebrating your return, anxious to catch up on all you have missed while you were on earth. The physical body remains on earth as the etheric body enters the gateway.

You have heard people say at the time of death, "Go into the light." The light they are referring to is a higher frequency than the physical body. Of course, your spirit is often light enough once you shed the earthly body.

The Healing Light

The etheric body is a body of energy that permeates the physical body, giving it sustenance, health, and vitality, without which the physical body could not be alive. The etheric body can retain unresolved emotions and thoughts. In addition, all life forms, including plants and animals, have etheric bodies for their health and survival.

My astral travel with beings of light prepared me to travel into the afterlife in order to be present for souls transitioning. I have observed that once through the gateway, souls are encircled by a healing light to assimilate them to their new surroundings and to shed their etheric bodies. This process clears the energy field to prepare for the life review. The life review is like watching a streaming video of your life. With the advantage of the powerful healing light, souls can accept and comprehend their own life journeys.

Prayers from the living can assist their loved ones in the transition into the afterlife to shed their etheric bodies, heal emotional and physical wounds, and clear the mind. You are not powerless; you can help your loved ones.

A client wanted to connect with her deceased father to find out whether he was okay. As I described my abilities earlier in this book, I can communicate with deceased souls. So I connected with her father as he described his experience transitioning from his body to the afterlife:

> It was like, I was neither dreaming or awake. I had no sense of my body. I floated into another dimension like when meditating. Loving beings of light surrounded me; there were no words shared between us. I just had a sense of love and of being weightless. I trusted them, and we moved effortlessly together toward the light. I am at peace.

Spirit guides, angels, your soul group, and you conduct a life review of every choice you made on earth and the effects of those choices on others. Time and space are earthly concepts. Our subtle energy bodies embody every memory in our lives. I learned about the life review by communicating with departed souls who explained to me what they had experienced.

There is no punishment, only love and understanding. It is a time to accept your mistakes, your shortcomings, and your faults to make room for possibilities and growth in the afterlife. This acceptance and understanding allows for an ascension to a higher frequency. Individuals who hold on to the traumas and dramas of their lives can take longer to pass through this stage. There is no time or space; however long it takes, it takes.

After the life review, you are reunited with your soul group. We are all unique frequencies of light who always were and always will be, so our loved ones will always recognize us in the afterlife. With the support of angels, soul group members, and spirit guides, it is decided where we will go next for more healing or learning. Once settled in, deceased souls can return to earth and leave messages. They have different abilities just like us: some can, and some cannot.

Souls must adjust their vibrations to return to earth. It can be difficult; often the best they can do is focus their energy in a beam of light to send a chill or vibration to our bodies, like the "holy shivers" or a tap on the forehead. As electrical beings they can manipulate the electricity of lights, remote controls, and cell phones.

Clients who come to see me often ask questions about their loved ones. The following are answers to frequently asked questions about the afterlife:

- You will see your loved ones again.
- They are safe, loved, and supported.
- They can see you and your family and are present for special events.
- They will leave you signs that they are around; be open to see them.
- You can call on your loved ones and ancestors for guidance; they are happy to help you.
- You do not bother them or prevent them from experiencing their journey.
- Souls near death often leave their bodies to enjoy the earthly plane a little longer.
- You have free choice to live your life as you want; it is okay to remarry or sell the house.

- Each soul continues to have free will and is not coerced.
- There is no time or space; time is not linear, and space is unlimited.

The conclusion is that as you embrace the afterlife and accept that consciousness is eternal, every choice becomes more relevant. The physical world can deceive us and lure us away from our true nature. When you open your mind that there is more to your existence than meets the eye, you change the lens through which you see the world.

A belief in the afterlife and the continuation of consciousness can ignite you to embrace who you really are, trust your intuition, and invite in your spirit guides. Who knows how your life and the world will change until you try? It is time to breathe deeply to know yourself and create a better world. You are divine light, and you come from universal light and love. The journey on earth is a temporary existence; our bodies die, and our spirits live on. We will all return to light one day.

Our loved ones who died often remind us to live our lives how we want to be remembered—as the caring, loving human beings that we are meant to be. The house, the cars, the jobs, and the vacations seem less important than finding our true selves and living a congruent life.

We do not have to wait until we die to reflect on our lives, to conduct our own life reviews, to heal wounds, to make course corrections, to forgive, to accept, to love more, to be present, and to live an authentic life. When you are in the present moment and live your life from your heart, you will find inner peace, joy and happiness.

A Poem from Tagore on "Immortality and Beyond"[16]

Can't You Hear Him
Have you not heard his silent steps?
At every moment and every age
Every day and every night
In the fragrant springtime and down the frozen path
In the rainy gloom of a summer storm
When his thunderous chariot passes overhead

---

[16] Deepak Chopra, *On the Shores of Eternity: Poems from Tagore on Immortality and Beyond* (Published by Harmony Books, New York, New York, 1999).

In sorrow after sorrow, joy after joy
That press upon my heart—
He comes, he comes, he ever comes ...

Death will come to all us, to all loved ones, pets, plants, and animals. No one can escape the ultimate truth that our physical existence will one day no longer exist as we know it. Death brings us closer to the reality that we are spiritual beings.

As Buddha said, "Death makes life happen by reminding us that our existence is temporary."

CHAPTER 8
Deceased Souls Who Speak to Me

During a healing energy session, a departed soul can grasp the opportunity to share a message with a loved one. These messages can heal unresolved issues that can lead to poor mental, physical, emotional, and spiritual health. I have been blessed to be present for such miracles and healing.

I would like to share some stories on the afterlife from clients who came to me for a healing energy session. Each individual I meet has his or her own story to tell, lessons to be learned, and wisdom to be gained that can ultimately be shared with others. These stories may help you to expand your view beyond that which you can see, taste, and feel in your physical reality.

A Shattered Heart Heals

A client was referred to me due to exhaustion that led to her taking a leave of absence from work. She said, "Western medicine could find nothing wrong, and yet I have an aching in my heart, exhaustion, and severe stomachaches." She was a beautiful, educated, successful woman in her forties. I asked her if anything had changed in her life when the pain began. She said, "My mother died from cancer six months ago. I adored my mother, and she adored me."

When I asked her about her belief in the afterlife, her eyes filled with tears as she said, "I believe in heaven and that my mother is in a better place. I do not understand why I am so exhausted. I cannot focus at work, and I have little energy for my daughter, whom I cherish." I asked about her mother's spiritual beliefs. She replied, "As a child of immigrant parents who had come to the United States in their early twenties, assimilation was important. The family became Christians."

As an energy healing practitioner, I have developed a fine-tuned system to read and interpret the energy field of a client and deceased souls. I closed my eyes and breathed in a few calming breaths to connect to my spirit, clearing my energy field first. Then, with full conscious attention, I observed a deep, gaping wound in the center of my client's chest. It looked as though she had been sliced wide open. The energy within her chest seemed to have ruptured and was leaking from her heart. I knew from my experience that it would require significant work to heal. I sensed that the pain in her heart and her mother were connected.

I then visualized her deceased mother to see where she was in her transition. The mother told me, "My husband insisted that we not stand out and stressed the importance of living the American dream. I conformed to my husband's wishes, as was my custom, and lived a happy American life." I observed in her energy field that, during her life in the United States, a silvery white energetic thread to her ancestors had gotten very thin. She berated herself, "I should have kept my practice and taught my daughter about her cultural traditions and ancestry. I do not deserve the elders' assistance."

The mother existed in a low vibrational environment in a state of confusion, her life force depleted. Two grim-faced elders in traditional clothing were nearby. My intuition told me that the mother had not received the traditional death ritual, was incapable of moving forward, and was reluctant to go with the elders. She was conservative, beautiful, kind, and intelligent in the physical world, as well as proud. Not feeling worthy of her traditional elders' assistance, she resisted and became stuck in nothingness.

I invited ancestors, spirit guides, ascended masters, and angels to bring light, love, and healing to assist. Through my clairvoyance, I was able to determine that the mother and daughter had been soul partners in many previous lives, making the *energetic cord*, a silvery white thread, between them strong. A miracle happened next, a very unusual occurrence of love, light, and hope. The daughter's soul joined the mother. I observed the following with my eyes closed, focusing all my energy on sending healing light to the pair. I could see clearly as though the scene was on a movie screen.

In the shadowy darkness, the daughter, appearing as a child dressed in traditional clothing, reached out to hold her mother's hand. This set a series of events into motion. Beautiful, colorful, varied scented flowers bloomed in slow motion as though the daughter was willing them to appear where there had been none moments before, only darkness. The daughter distracted her mother by telling her to gaze at the colorful blooming flowers and step onto the flat slate stones in her path. In silence they walked along the stone path; with each step, the next stone materialized. The path wound through a beautiful garden and led to a thousand ancient stone steps on the side of a steep mountain. The blue sky above was scattered with white clouds amid the purest air one could breathe, yet no one needed a breath.

The time spent in the darkness had depleted the mother's life force. After a few steps her shoulders slumped as though she would give up. At that moment, magically, they both became as light as air as their soul bodies floated above the steps, joining the two elders in the plane of healing at the top of the mountain. The elders performed their ritual at an altar that included incense, fruit, statues, and candles. She was reunited with many spiritual ancestors who had come to pray. Soon she was in her vibrant spiritual body.

As her mother ascended, the daughter's chest miraculously healed. I worked to seal the perimeter to prevent any more leaking energy. Fearlessly, the daughter's soul did not hesitate to support her mother. It was as though she remembered the journey into the afterlife and could guide her. The mother and daughter had lived many lives together.

Once settled in the afterlife, the mother asked me to direct her daughter to create an altar, specifically asking her to place a two-by-three-inch picture of the mother's face with her eyes looking straight out and a smile on her face. The mother promised to always be near and to visit her in a dream in the coming months. She expressed a desire for her granddaughter to know the family customs. The daughter agreed to ask her aunts about their cultural traditions and to incorporate them into her life and her daughter's.

The daughter inhaled full, deep breaths without pain in her chest for the first time in six months. This was an unusual story where a wound was so deep in an individual who was grieving that it caused physical exhaustion and pain. I was blessed and honored to be present for a miracle.

The moral of the story is that the universe is a field of particles that are connected in the physical and nonphysical dimensions (space) and in a linear and a nonlinear continuum (time). Our perceptions and beliefs have immense power to influence our health and destiny in this world and beyond. There is no separation between us and the afterlife, only perceived separation. We are all one.

Fishing with My Father

A man in his midsixties came to me for a healing energy session. He had a date set for retirement and wasn't convinced that it was a good idea. He didn't know what to do and thought an energy balancing might be helpful. The goal of the session was for overall health and vitality as he entered retirement.

The session went smoothly. He looked deeply relaxed as I moved my hands over his body and transmitted healing energy for his highest possibilities and best good. At the end of the session, he sat straight up on the side of the table beaming from ear to ear. He said, "My father has been dead for forty years, and he was talking to me as clearly as if he was standing in front of me." He said, "I believe in heaven, but I have never connected with my father. This is a gift beyond my expectations." With tears in his eyes, he described the scene: "I was fishing with my father, and our conversation about my commencing retirement was amazing. I am confident that this is the right time for retirement, and I will enjoy myself."

The moral of the story is that our loved ones are always with us and can still provide wisdom exactly at the right time. A simple message from his father changed this man's outlook on retirement.

No, No, Dear, I Am All Right

A woman in her sixties came for a healing energy session to bring a little more zest to her life. She told me, "The man of my dreams and lifetime companion died after an illness with cancer. I am lost without him in my quiet moments at home at night. I keep myself busy with activities, needlepoint, friends, and travel during the day." During the session, I got goose bumps and the holy shivers as I sensed the presence of male energy and overwhelming unconditional love. As I moved around the room, I could still sense the energy as it had filled the room. I could tell his love for his wife was profound.

He said, "Find a companion, a nice man to cuddle you at night, dear."

"No," she said, "I never want to sleep with anyone other than you."

"How about a man who can change light bulbs for you, dear?"

"No," she said emphatically, "I can find a friend to help me."

He offered, "How about a pet, a dog or cat?"

"No, no," she insisted. "I don't need more work, and I like to travel with my friends."

Persistently trying to help, he said, "How about a stuffed animal?"

"No, I wouldn't feel comfortable with a stuffed animal at my age. I am just lonely at night. I miss you at night when I go to bed. Really, I am fine."

The next night at bingo, her cards were close to winning all night. It was not until the last card of the night when she yelled, "Bingo!" She won a stuffed dog. She named the dog Penelope, and it sleeps on her bed. Penelope reminds her that her deceased husband is watching over her and that she is not alone.

The moral of the story is that you never know how a deceased loved one will let you know they are near, so be open to a miracle. Every day is a new day, so get up, get dressed, show up, and see what happens. You can be curious and open about your world because deceased souls are often persistent, loving, and surprising. Keep your eyes open!

Could You Hate a Four-Year-Old Boy?

A retired woman came to me for a healing energy session because she lacked joy even though she had a great life. She described her life, saying, "I have a loving family, friends, financial security, extensive travel, a comfortable home, and a strong spiritual practice. But something is missing. I have worked hard and want to find joy in my life and discover my true purpose. I seek joy in simple things. I am not asking for a lot. I just want to feel joy."

She expected to find joy in retirement, but to her surprise, after a year of retirement joy has eluded her. In my mind's eye, with my eyes closed and full conscious attention, I observed intense emotions anchored in her throat, heart, and lower back causing a disruption in her energy field and physical pain in her legs. I told her that I sensed she had buried strong anger and hate in her body. She said, "I am confused. I just told you my life is good."

After a pause, she said, "I have not thought about this for a long time. I thought I had let it go, but I just saw my first husband's sister, and she reminded me of all this." She cried, "I am still in pain. I hate my ex-husband's father. He ruined my husband's life, my life, and our children's. I do not hate my husband anymore, just his father."

She added, "I finally realized that it was not my ex-husband's fault. His father was abusive. He would wake him at night to beat him for no reason and hold a knife to his mother's throat. He destroyed my ex-husband. I hate no one, but I hate him. He ruined our daughter's life through his alcoholism and brutality too. He died decades ago, but I cannot forgive him even though I am a spiritual person."

I asked cautiously as she was so adamant, "What do you hate? Do you hate the image of this man who no longer exists? An illusion of the physical body of a man that is gone? We are all beings of divine light, and he is too. He left his physical body on earth and entered the afterlife to heal, learn, forgive, and be forgiven. His essence is no longer the man you hated."

I explained, "I believe that all of us do the best we can with our upbringing, experiences, addictions, knowledge, and lack of support. If he had been loved by his parents, maybe he would not have done what he did." I suggested that we send light and love to her father-in-law for his highest good.

She said, "I cannot. He was so horrible." I could not assuage her. Unfortunately, the joy and pleasure she seeks will continue to be filtered by this hate.

Through my clairvoyance, I connected to the deceased soul of her ex-husband's father. However, the deceased soul was no longer in the afterlife. He had returned to earth with a mission to love and to be loved. He appeared as a toddler dressed in modern clothing on a living room floor playing with toy cars and blocks with his younger sisters—a soul hopeful for a better life. He peered over his shoulder at me with pleading eyes and said, "Shield me from this woman's hate and give me a chance to experience love." I filled the child with light and love, creating a protective shield.

The woman's hatred sailed through time and space to this child's soul. The strength of her negative energy that she was intentionally sending to him transcended time and space. Although he had been dead for decades, the hate she has for him still reaches him. She could endanger him and repeat this ugly pattern of abuse. Who in your life has played the antagonist for you? Souls can play a role in our evolving consciousness that at the time seems harsh. I tried to encourage her to embrace what she had learned about herself and her ability to love and accept her life as it was.

The moral of the story is that, if you hate someone, I implore you to release the anger you have. And, if you can, open your heart and send light and love to them so that we can stop this crazy cycle of hatred to allow rebirth and to instill hope for all of us to have a better life. The act of forgiveness and acceptance is the way we heal.

An Old Soul Returns with a Mission

A friend came to me to better understand how an eleven-year-old boy who loved life, his family, and everyone he met could commit suicide. He had been proud of who he was and expressed himself freely, but he was openly gay and subsequently bullied at school and on social media. Privately at home he felt the pain, hiding it from his family. One day it became too much, and he shot himself.

My friend knew this family well. The boy's parents were beside themselves wondering what they could have done differently to save their son. His parents and grandparents loved him, all of him, and would have done anything to make the world better for him. The incident created a flurry in the media that led to changes at his school.

The family was inconsolable and could not understand how this had happened. I contacted the soul of the boy to see if I could get some answers. I was surprised. I can never predict what I will encounter from a soul in the afterlife. The image I saw was a wise, ancient man with a long white beard, long hair, and solemn face. The man explained that he had chosen to live a short life to teach others about being open-minded and to bring awareness to a community. He had selflessly sacrificed his young life on earth. He knew that he would return to the afterlife in his true essence. His unconditional love for humanity and a selfless act of kindness gave him courage.

The moral of the story is that we may never know why people we love die. We can choose to honor their journeys and courage to live the lives they chose, freeing us to live our lives too. All consciousness transcends time, space, and the physical body of a human being. An earth experience is temporary.

The conclusion is that our physical reality is too limited to explain all things. I tell clients to take the messages that come and let them set for a bit. The interpretation is really up to them. Each and every human living on earth is a soul with its own journey. There is so much more than we will ever understand about a soul's journey. Your loved ones in the afterlife are the sum total of every life they have ever lived. They will always remember you and greet you when you return to the afterlife. You are more than this one life, as well. Your soul's consciousness is embedded in your body and can be accessed with your intuition and guidance from your spirit guides.

Life should not be about struggling against all odds to survive. Life is to be embraced and lived. May this be your truth. Peace, peace, peace. *Shanti, Shanti, Shanti.*

CHAPTER 9
Your Loved Ones in the Afterlife

Stories from souls in the afterlife illustrate how close your loved ones might be. The knowledge that the space between the physical world and the afterlife is not such a big chasm after all can be comforting. Your loved ones are closer than you think, although where they are and what they are doing is a mystery.

In the afterlife, there is much to do, nothing to do, much to learn, and nothing to learn in a dimension where there is no time, space, or gravity. We know other galaxies exist, yet we cannot reach them due to the earthly limitations of travel. In the afterlife, you are no longer limited by your physical body or geography. You are simply a being of light, like a star. Each and every one of us has a unique frequency of light that cannot be created or destroyed. We always were and always will be unique beings of light.

Light travels at a constant, finite speed of 186,000 miles per second. If you could travel at the speed of light, you would be able to circumnavigate the globe approximately seven and a half times in one second. Meanwhile, a person flying at an average speed of about 500 miles per hour would cross the continental United States once in four hours or circle the planet once in just over fifty hours.[17]

At what speed can a being of light travel? The speed of light is known, but what if there are other speeds that science cannot detect? Science has proved that light travels millions of miles from distant stars. How far beings of light can travel in space is a mystery. Our loved ones in the afterlife have

---

[17] *LTP*, "How 'Fast' Is the Speed of Light?" Accessed November 11, 2018, https://www.grc.nasa.gov/www/k-12/Numbers/Math/Mathematical_Thinking/how_fast_is_the_speed.htm

limitless abilities to travel to earth and find you, your children, and loved ones. As with your spirit guides, you can ask them for help too.

It is my belief that a soul's experience on earth is an infinitesimally small piece of a much bigger puzzle of many soul lives. When a soul returns to the afterlife, there is an attempt to balance all experiences in their many lives as they evolve.

As a being of light, there is no urgency to complete a task in the afterlife. Mystics and people in ancient civilizations can connect with souls. And you can too if you have recognized a loved one in a dream or vision.

The afterlife holds many possibilities for existence on planes called the planes of light. *The Tibetan Book of the Dead*[18] and many scholars talk about twelve planes of light and generally agree on their characteristics. No one really knows the number of planes or dimensions available to us across the galaxies. The truth is there could be limitless planes of light in the universe. A multiverse of beings and dimensions could exist.

Where your loved ones are and what they are doing is an unknown—and quite frankly may be none of your business. You could just let them be and instead focus your curiosity on living your life to its fullest. Yet it is so heartwarming to connect with their love that is always available. So why not ask? They will be there for you.

Somewhere in the afterlife, souls are either busy or at rest; souls have free will to choose. They are not coerced. Teachers assist in their learning. For example, one of the lessons may be to embody wisdom. A wise person learns to be impeccable with his or her words, which is a higher skill than just being honest. You can be honest and still hurt someone with your words. A wise person uses words carefully to convey difficult messages with compassion so that they are received and heard.

You may ask what happens to all those "bad" people who die—the terrorists, rapists, and murderers. They are all accepted into the afterlife and have the same options available to them. We are unique frequencies of light and part of the universal consciousness. There is no separation on earth or in the afterlife. Some souls will agree to come back to earth in order to face their responsibilities by accepting a difficult life and fulfill karma.

Remember, the reasons that humans live the lives they do are affected

---

[18] Padma Sambhava

by many factors. Karma balances "good" and "bad" through experiences on earth. Even souls who exhibited bad behavior and made choices against the good of mankind have an inner light that is seeking to be whole. When you send light and love to those who do bad things, it may help them to make better choices.

When you remember a loved one's violent, horrific, or tragic death and attach emotion to the memory, you can cause harm to the deceased soul. They receive your thoughts in energy waves of subatomic particles. People who bled to death are not still bleeding to death. People who died of cancer do not still have cancer. They have no body at all. Where you put your thoughts is where the energy flows, so be mindful and send love.

The imprint of a tragic story that you play over and over in your mind can cause endless suffering for you too. When you think of an event with emotion, your body does not know it is not happening now. The body responds as though it is happening and causes discord in your mental, physical, and spiritual bodies. Your thoughts can create more suffering, or they can create more healing. Instead you can send light and love to heal and honor your loved ones and yourself. Celebrations of life are replacing traditional funerals for this very reason.

It is important to remember that the body died but the spirit does not end. The spirit lives on; nothing can destroy the spirit. The spirit is whole, perfect, and complete in its essence of divine light. If you are angry about the circumstances of a death and blame caregivers, health-care workers, or family members, you may hold onto anger, hate, and fear. Trauma, chronic diseases, accidents, and violent acts can lead to anger too.

Yes, there are bad people who do bad things and unfortunate events that occur, but anger adds fuel to the fire. And the person experiencing the anger experiences the fire and limits his or her own life force. If possible, we need to send love to those who harmed our loved ones so that they feel love and may not harm anyone else. Karma is an interesting concept. The rebalancing of the universe happens at a level we cannot see, but rebalance it does.

Sometimes a loved one dies to bring more light to the afterlife in order to guide other souls there. The afterlife is not separate from earth; we need more light everywhere. I have met souls who believed they could do more to help their loved ones in spirit form than in human form. The releasing of souls back to the afterlife brings more light to heal departed souls, too.

In a past-life recall, I was in a village in Ireland, and warriors were killing everyone to take over our land. I died first so that I could reach my hand down and assist my family into the light. Another time, a client whose father had died in his fifties came to me for healing. The father's spirit explained to me that he was deeply spiritual, worked hard at his career, and loved his family, and yet he was not able to incorporate a ministry on earth. He had a vocation to serve others. He explained to me that he could reach so many more people as a spirit and could teach souls in the afterlife to send love to the earth. The afterlife needed another teacher, and he agreed to the task. His daughter felt relieved that he was providing such a service.

I have heard so many stories from souls; there is no way to know all the possibilities with our limited human minds. Try to be open to miracles beyond what you can see and comprehend. Miracles are everywhere— always have and always will be. All possibilities already exist at the same time.

In conclusion, can you remember an event in your life that lasted but one minute and changed the shape of your future? Souls too can have an experience in the afterlife that can change them forever. Those who made poor choices or died tragically on earth can heal with support and love. The afterlife is dynamic, and souls are evolving. Your loved ones are evolving too.

An understanding of the afterlife and souls who exist there can free us from our burden of grief and fear. Souls in the afterlife are having the experience they are supposed to be having so that they can evolve consciousness, rest, heal and build the capacity to love the world. When in doubt, trust that your loved ones are exactly where they are supposed to be. Most likely, they are.

CHAPTER 10
A Soul Returns to Earth

What is gravity, and why do we sleep? Many wonders of nature remain a mystery to us. So, too, is the mystery of a soul's journey back to earth. Imagine the universe as one vibrating, oscillating unit of stars. On a clear night in the country away from city lights, you can see thousands of stars in the night sky. Some stars we cannot see; the universe is infinite. You too are a star, a true beacon of light, albeit infinitesimally small.

The human race in its entirety is only a drop in the universal consciousness. And yet our spirits are protected by a great cosmic structure that cannot be created or destroyed, just as energy cannot be created or destroyed.

A soul agrees to incarnate after a conversation with its spirit guides, soul group, and earth parents. A soul contract is prepared and agreed upon prior to the birth based on opportunities to learn earth lessons and share intrinsic gifts with the world. Usually a soul enters around the sixteenth to nineteenth week of gestation, the time of quickening, or fetal movement. Most often souls do not hang out in the womb while the cells are replicating. There are no lessons to learn during that time.

A mystical truth is that the greater cosmos is filled with light, love, and energy. You came from light, and you are light. Your birth experience and the family dynamics you experience as a child cannot separate you from the light. We are protected by the great universal light. We are all worthy of love; it is a mystical law. The sun shines for all of us. We are neither deserving nor undeserving; it just is. We are all worthy, and we are all loved in this and every moment.

When you manifest your soul's desire, you can bring a sense of belonging, peace, and acceptance to your life. It is work to understand who you are at the human level and to understand your personality, strengths, challenges, and soul's desire. It takes time, intention, and a full conscious awareness to manifest the deepest desires of your soul. There is help from your intuition and your spirit guides; all you need to do is listen. A key to understanding the subtle wisdom, love, and support available to us starts with knowing that we are not separate; we are all connected. We are, we always have been, and we always will be.

Our unique essence of light is eternal. In the same way I can interpret the energy field of a deceased loved one, I can receive information from a living soul whose thoughts have not yet or are unable to reach conscious awareness. I first developed this skill as a pediatric nurse with children who were transitioning into the afterlife. When I share information with loved ones, they often respond that they already knew the information to be true in their heart. The mind does not have access to this information; the heart does. The mind tries to find reasons to answer the questions "Why?" and "What can I do to fix things?" As you read the story below, you will see that the grandmother knew in her heart the truth, yet hearing it provided her great comfort.

A Grief-Stricken Grandmother

A grandmother came to me for a healing energy session to relieve the anxiety and stress she had regarding her daughter's and grandson's situation. Her health was suffering, she could not sleep, and she made poor diet choices. She said, "I need to be healthy to help my family." Her four-year-old grandson had been diagnosed with rare cancerous tumors in his brain as well as functional, cognitive, and developmental delays with a life expectancy of twenty years. The woman exclaimed, "How could such an innocent young boy have such a horrible disease? And my daughter is such a beautiful woman. This is consuming her life." She said, "My daughter gets so upset at the nurses and doctors. They don't coordinate his care. They make mistakes. She just cannot take it anymore. They tell me there are some experimental studies we could try. There are no promises. She doesn't know what to do, and she is a single mother." The grandmother told me, "This young boy can light up a room with his love for life. He seems to accept his challenges."

As always, I prepared for the session by clearing my mind, body, and spirit and inviting in the light, love, and energy of the earth and the cosmos above for the highest possibility and best good. The grandchild lived over a thousand miles away, which in spirit and energy is a small distance. The grandmother had an energy cord to her grandson. I followed the energy in my mind's eye to ask the child how he was doing and interpret his energy field. A vision of a small boy in his room at home came to me; he was pale, weak, and content.

During the healing energy session, the spirit of the child asked me to tell his mom, "I want to feel loved and to be held. I chose you for your love. Thank you for being my mom." He said, "I just want to be loved unconditionally. I do not want to play sports or anything like other children do. I came to earth to bask in your love. That is enough. I agreed to a short life and will return to the afterlife filled with more light. I am happy as I am; just love me. I am not suffering. I am exactly where I am supposed to be. Your grief is not helping me. Please send me light and love so that I can be as healthy as I can be while I am here."

The only thing he asked was not to be poked or prodded by the doctors any more than necessary. "Just let me be me. Love me as I am. I love you, too, Grandma."

The moral of the story is that the mother's displaced anger at the health-care professionals and an inefficient system did not help. The mother and grandmother had an idea in their minds about who and what this boy should be; their egos led the way instead of their beautiful, loving hearts. The grandmother told me that she would love him just as he was and tell her daughter about our session. The adults did not need to lament. Children often teach us to embrace life and to enjoy the blessings they bring. The child asked his family to release their regrets and to love him. This soul had come to earth to experience love and Mother Earth energy.

***

I was reminded of the movie *Arrival*, in which the mother knew her daughter would have cancer and chose to have her anyway. She embraced the blessing of the love between them, believing it was better to have loved and lost than to never have loved the child. Surely this is not a sentiment that everyone would embrace, but it certainly brings more light to the world.

Every soul is a unique being of light, independent, free, and responsible for planning its life lessons, including the family into which it is born. It is not always a perfect match, but an attempt is made to support the soul lessons that are being sought to balance karma and to evolve consciousness.

The families into which you are born may fulfill a contract that you do not understand. Parents do not always provide the love and nurturing that is ideal. Humans depend on the family unit for survival and seek attachments to create a sense of safety and security, though in reality this may not be the case.

Humans do have an innate ability to love. However, too often parents can misplace this ability to give unconditional love on their children due to their childhood traumas. The most common reason I have heard from souls born into difficult childhoods is to conquer the challenge of loving themselves unconditionally and not to be dependent on the external world for love. Once they love themselves, they love the world more. The following is such a story.

A Boy's Father Was Abusive

An elderly man came to me for a session to better understand his difficult childhood. His father was abusive verbally and chastised him for his behavior when he expressed his opinions. He said, "My father never loved me." In a session, his deceased father communicated to his son, "I love you, and we have lived many lives together. In this life I agreed to be hard on you so that you could learn to love yourself more. I was your teacher."

The son exclaimed, "Boy, you did a great job being a jerk! You were really hard on me. I did learn, though. Thank you."

The father said, "I knew you could do it. I love you."

The moral of the story is that it is possible to rise above an earthly experience into the midst of spirit to gain a new understanding of our physical reality. There may be more than meets the eye. Your parents and families may not be the source of love that you seek. Try to be open to the blessings coming toward you from other experiences and people in the world. Love comes from many sources when we are open. A mystical truth is that you came from light and you are light. Your birth experience or the family dynamics you experience as a child cannot separate you from the light.

***

A soul is waiting in the wings to be called into life as a human egg and sperm unite. It is never one thing or one reason that things happen as they do. It is a mystery. If a soul decides it is not ready to come or the timing is not right, a pregnancy may be aborted. Most of us will never know the reason a miscarriage occurs. Nothing is wrong with you if you have a miscarriage. A million things have to go right for a pregnancy to result in a human being; it is a miracle of cell growth, separation, and division. A soul seeking an earthly experience will find an earthly experience. The physical cells die while the spirit lives on.

A new life incarnates after much consideration from souls, guides, ancestors, birth and earth parents, and even siblings. A fractured maternal-child bond can be daunting and cause a lifetime of bewilderment, pain, and fear. In a healing energy session, a parent, a child, a baby, or a soul separated in some way can come through with his or her side of the story. Each soul has its own story, and it may have nothing to do with you. The following stories of conversation with these souls can be magical and provide healing.

Remember the Joy

A woman approached after a lecture on understanding the afterlife. She said, "I lost a baby at the end of the first trimester. Do you think you could check in on her? I get so depressed and sad every time I think about the baby. It has been more than thirty years." A spirit popped in during our discussion to say, "I just agreed to come to show you that you have the capacity to love." The fairy-like energy flitted about, all shiny, light, and glowing, and enthusiastically said, "Remember the joy you felt when you found out you were pregnant. I wanted you to feel joy so that you could see that you have the capacity for joy. I have always been with you. I am your spirit guide. I remind you to laugh, play, and enjoy your life, to lighten up. You know me, do you not?" She excitedly said, "Yes! Yes, I know you." She had no idea her spirit guide and the departed baby were connected. The spirit guide told her, "I enjoy being with you from the spirit world, and I did not choose to be incarnated. I didn't want the difficult earth experience; I just wanted to be with you. Motherhood is only one of the many ways to experience love and joy."

The moral of the story is that the spirit guide asked that she accept that everyone is not intended to be an earthly mother. There are many ways to send and receive love and to share our gifts with the world.

Heal Yourself First

A thirty-one-year-old woman came to a healing energy session to reduce anxiety resulting from a miscarriage at the end of the first trimester. Her goal for the session was to release the anger at herself for losing the baby and to release the anxiety surrounding getting pregnant. She told me, "I was diagnosed with major clinical depression requiring therapy and medication. My career is in limbo, and the tension in my marriage is unbearable. I must have done something wrong, or something is wrong with me. I will probably never have a baby, and my life will never be complete." She added, "I have so much love to give a baby, and everything in my life will turn around. My friends are having babies and are so happy. I want to be happy too."

She said, "I became obsessed about getting pregnant. I measure my temperature, monitor my menstrual cycle, schedule intercourse, eat healthy, and exercise. This additional anxiety and stress is overwhelming."

First of all, I told her, "A million things have to go right to create the miracle of a baby." I tried to assure her that the miscarriage was not her fault; things happen. And the effect of her anger and overzealous behavior could actually energetically block her success at becoming pregnant.

As always, I prepared for the session by clearing my mind, body, and spirit and inviting in the light, love, and energy of the earth and the cosmos above and asked for the highest possibility and best good. I guided her in a meditation to enhance relaxation. As she quietly rested, I held my hands over her body to send light and love into her body and the field around her body. I could see her body relax, and her breathing slowed. I sensed that her field was clear.

Although there was no change in the temperature of the room, a pocket of air in the room felt freezing cold. You know what it is like in a lake when you float over a cold spring and the water is really cold? It was like that in this one area of the room. It was then that I had a vision. An infant male was being comforted by a lovely older woman who was doting on the baby. I could sense so much love and care between them. As I described the vision to my client, she said, "That could be my maternal grandmother. It sounds like her. She loves me, and she loves babies."

The message I received from the soul waiting in the wings to be born was, "I would like for you to be my mother when you are ready." The maternal grandmother told her, "The more you love yourself, the more love you will have for this baby coming into the world."

My client was so excited. "What do I have to do?"

I explained to her that the limiting self-talk and focus on procreating hindered the flow of energy through her body. I recommended creative activities, walks in nature, and imagining fairies and pixies playing among the flowers and plants. This would not work for everyone, but I sensed it would work for her. She understood that wonder and imagination would enhance the flow of energy in her body. I encouraged her to do the best she could to relax, enjoy her life, love her life, and expect a miracle. I taught her some self-care techniques to handle anxiety that I will share in the appendix.

The moral of the story is that you must love and value yourself in order to have the love to give another human being. Each soul carries its own light, love, and energy into the world to share with its earth family. You cannot expect a baby to make you happy and fix your problems of self-esteem. Those of you who are parents know that things get more complicated in real life. The power of true love for self and others comes in handy.

A Mother Torn

A woman in her fifties with a big smile, bounce in her step, and gregarious attitude entered my healing energy room excited and talkative about her work. She said, "I am so blessed to have a career that is so rewarding. I love to sing and dance in musicals at theaters across the region." She indicated that she has had energy work before and was looking for a general balancing of her energy system. She said, "I get tired more easily than I used to. I need more stamina. Can you help me out?"

As I prepared for the energy session, I sensed blocked energy in her lower body, which often indicates a lack of safety and a sense of belonging in the world. When I told her this and asked if she had any idea why this may be true, she teared up and said, "I block out the anger when I perform. The only time I am happy is when I am singing on stage." This anger has plagued her for her entire life. She said, "I perform because it is make-believe. I can be happy and complete in the moment. I was adopted. My mother abandoned me, and I am angry. My adoptive parents told me the doctor convinced her to give me up. She was young, single, had a hopeful career as an entertainer, and limited resources of time and money to care for an infant. The father was not involved. They were at the hospital within twenty-four hours of my birth to get me. I feel like I was taken from my mother who loved me."

I guided her in a meditation to enhance relaxation, dimmed the lights, and covered her with a light sheet. She relaxed into the table easily as I worked to release the blocked energy with my hands over her body and full conscious intention. As her energy cleared, the soul of her birth mother appeared in a vision to me. The birth mother expressed to me, "I was torn. I dearly love my daughter and want the best for her. I had a career ahead of me that may not have happened if I was distracted by a baby." Then, speaking to the daughter, "I loved you more than myself. It was a difficult decision. I thought you would be so fortunate and blessed to have such a good family to take care of you. I believed at the time that the adoptive family would do better than I could, with so few resources. I sensed you are a strong person and you would always land on your own two feet. And you did."

The birth mother went on to say, "We are soul sisters; we are not mother and daughter. Please do not have any hard feelings. Enjoy your life and find the joy you are meant to embrace. I hope that you can release this burden of abandonment. I have always sent you my love. You have never been alone. You are loved, and you have always been loved. We will meet again. Choose life and choose joy." These words consoled her, and she knew they were true.

She said, "I always felt that my mother loved me. I could not understand why she didn't want me. What I did not realize is that she was actually sending me love the whole time."

The moral of the story is that we are all loved, and we are all connected. Your birth mother can still love you and send you love even though she gave you up for adoption. Let go of the fear that can limit your ability to embrace the life you are meant to live. Trust that you are divinely loved and never alone.

A Miracle from around the World

A friend shared her story of adoption and how she quickly traveled around the world to receive her son into her family. She said, "I longed to be a mother and prayed for a child." The conductor in the invisible world orchestrated souls from around the world. They never met yet had a common goal for the health and well-being of this soul entering the earthly plane. The biological mother was loving, kind, and wanted the best for her special child who she could not afford to raise. She was honored to bring this soul into the world for his earthly experience, trusting the earth mother would love him and care for him unconditionally.

Energetic trails of prayers were created by the birth and the adoptive mother. They were both assisted by spirit guides. Through their intentions and love, I was able to connect with the triad of baby, birth mother, and earth mother with their benevolent guides and angels. This pack agreed to carry out their roles before the baby was born. The immense love the earth mother had was sent into the cosmic energy field and found a soul wandering in the Other World searching for a mother to raise him. The soul felt the strong love from the adoptive mother and found a way to be born where she would find him. All happened in the invisible world of love, grace, and intention. No mistakes are made in these situations. Miracles happen every day that are a blessing for all.

The moral of the story is that I believe that this arrangement happens more than we will ever know. There is more happening behind the scenes then we will ever be able to comprehend. If you are adopted, you can choose to be in the wonderment of your adoptive family and release the need to know more about your birth parents. Adoption can bring souls together when the earthly body cannot. Adopted children can enjoy the union of love and light. It is a blessing!

Not in the Obituary

A woman came for a healing energy session and told me, "I have a happy life, family, and a successful career as a psychotherapist. I feel blessed for my contributions to heal so many in my work. I am anticipating my retirement. Unfortunately, my knees are painful and swollen, making it difficult to walk. I want to heal my legs so that I can travel."

The energy flowing through her legs was compromised, and her heart felt heavy and wounded. When I asked her, "Is there anything you may be holding in your heart?" she said no. I asked the question many ways, but she was adamant: "No, I love the world, and I have a blessed life." I sensed her heart was stiff and shrunken from the time of her birth and shared this with her.

She said, "I was adopted at birth by a loving family. All is good. I even found my birth parents in my forties. My birth parents were engaged when I was born and later married, having four more children. I am the oldest. We are very similar in many ways. It's so much fun to have them in my life. It is a really good story."

The heart center was severely compromised, so I asked if there was anything else that would cause the heart to be so hardened. She said, "Wait a minute. I love my family, but I have not spoken to my birth mother in two years. I hate her. I thought I had let it go. She never accepted me as her daughter." The mother at eighty-eight years old had composed her own obituary, adamant that her adopted daughter not be mentioned. She said, "It is my life, and no one needs to know about her. She was never part of my life." The birth mother was in her nineties, and the division between them was severe. There was no contact. Her brother told her not to worry because she would be in the obituary, but it did not matter; the hurt was deep. An old wound festered beneath consciousness, creating a crevice deep in the left side of her heart.

Through my clairvoyance, I met with the aging mother. She explained,

"The social status of my family in the forties would not support my pregnancy. I left town to have the baby in secret. It disrupted my college to avoid a scandal to my family. I could not bear to feel the shame, pain, blame, powerlessness, and anger and bottled it up. I was angry that I could never really feel joy because of what I did and who I was. What a mistake in life that kept me from experiencing joy. Why would I want to be reminded of that time in my life?" I sent her love, light, and healing so that she may love herself, her choices, and her daughter to heal prior to her transition.

My client accepted the explanation I had received and chose to love herself enough to let go of her need for her mother's love. She consciously chose life and joy. She accepted that her mother had done the best she could at the time and that it was not personal. The woman got up off the table almost jumping for joy, saying, "I feel so light, and my legs do not hurt for the first time in six months." She almost floated out of the room. One day she may send love to her mother. Who knows?

The moral of the story is that we do not need the love of our birth mothers because there is so much love available to us in the world. Holding onto anger can cause unnecessary bitterness among family members. It takes a bigger person to see the higher ground, to forgive, and to love.

There is no reason good enough not to be in your power to live an authentic, rich, meaningful life. No matter your birth journey or life path, there is always hope and healing when you connect with your unique light within and infinite universal love. During your darkest time, you can find peace within one moment and then take a step in any direction. You will not know until you try.

***

The truth is that you are a soul having an earthly experience, and the challenge is to temper the ego with your soul. The ego is an inner voice that needs to be differentiated from the calling of the soul. Earthly responsibilities and teachings from childhood and our culture to do, achieve, master, get ahead, and make more money are based on the ego. The ego longs for what is missing or needs fixing. There is a wanting for objects, better jobs, and better homes. This leads to striving and a discontentment that results in a disconnect between what the mind thinks it wants and what the soul desires. The soul enters this incarnation with a knowing of a desire to evolve consciousness.

The mind does not like not knowing the answers to your questions, so it imagines answers, thus creating fear and unlikely scenarios. The ego can get involved in defining what is right, fair, or just, further causing distress and suffering and creating a loop of purposeless thoughts. These thoughts can lead to distressing emotions and cloud your intuition. You can choose to trust your intuition and messages from your guides to end this cycle.

Although there is nothing wrong with your ego, it is how you choose to use your ego that really matters. The ego may strive for a sports car and think, *I will enjoy driving the car around. Everyone will see me and wonder how I manifested this car.* The story about the car is fun at first, but then the story gets old and it becomes less fun to drive around and people get used to seeing you and no longer comment about what a cool car it is. Sometimes satisfying the ego gets the thought of the car out of your head so you can move on to soul work.

The ego does not have the same level of fulfillment, longevity, or sustainability as the desire of the soul. The following is a common story of the struggle between the ego and the soul and how our external world can distract us from our true self.

The following stories are from healing energy sessions with individuals who became distracted by their egos and experienced stress and anxiety as a result. I share these stories to show you how you can heal too.

Disconnected from the Soul

A stunningly beautiful, successful, overwhelmed woman dealing with competing priorities—a high-pressure career, large home, and young family—and the recent death of her father came to see me. She exercised regularly, ate healthily, drank in moderation, was married, and traveled frequently for her career. She had a loving, supportive family and many friends. She said, "I cannot stop my racing mind. I have so much to do. I have a busy life and want to enjoy it. I am anxious, irritable with my family and friends, and cannot sleep. It is hard to enjoy my life when I am so anxious." She asked, "Can you clear my mind so that I can relax?"

My intuitive assessment revealed that her mind was congested from overthinking and the energy in her throat was compromised. The energy centers in her stomach and chest were overstimulated from powering through her life and from being hard on herself for not meeting her high expectations. Most importantly, she was not grounded and not connected to her higher self. She was physically healthy yet spiritually disconnected. Spirit guides were in the background—not uninterested but not engaged due to the client's lack of connection or knowledge of their existence. Their soft, quiet voices could not be heard above the din of her mind.

The overthinking, planning, and doing prevent the higher self from peeking through. She would benefit from quiet time, pure rest, and relaxation to clear her mind and allow new ideas and thoughts to come through. A time to pose deep, inner questions would bring more meaning to her life, such as *Why am I here? Who am I? Where am I going next? What is inviting me? What am I being drawn to? What ignites my soul?*

Her mind said, *I think I am supposed to do this, achieve that, dress like this, say this and that, be here and there* and before she knew it, there was no time left to just be who she really was. The mind created a loop of its own, thus limiting the expansion of the true self. The mind and ego were stuck in this loop, causing congestion in the abdomen.

The ego is louder than the soul when you focus on bringing home the bacon. Also, into how many social engagements can you make a spectacular entrance carrying a perfect dish and a genuine smile? As an overachiever on the earthly plane, she sought recognition and was driven to succeed at all costs. No fight was too frightening to take on, and there was no word for *surrender* in her vocabulary. She was not alone—many men and women in the world get lost in the chase for more money, more stuff, more recognition, and more of more.

It is not sustainable to live in the world of the ego. For example, driving a new car feels good at first and then it gets old. The soul wants to be more current with who you are becoming than who you have been. The disconnect between the soul and the ego builds dis-ease in the subtle energy bodies and can lead to illness, depression, anger, resentment, or even a desire to run away from home.

When the ego takes over the human experience, souls feel lost, unfulfilled, and alone. My suggestions for her were to take the time to tune into her heart and become curious about the desire of her soul.

I let her know that when she lets go of striving, if only for a moment, to be at rest, her mind would clear, her emotions would calm, and her soul could emerge. The inner voice of her soul could speak and let her know what would sustain and nourish her mind, body, and spirit as she basked in the peacefulness of her soul at rest. From this place of calm, she could create a life aligned with her true nature.

During the healing energy session, I held my hands over her heart and transmitted eternal, infinite love from the violet and emerald rays. I invited her spirit guides to be more present so that she could feel their love. I sensed that she was an old, wise soul, a brilliant being of light. I also sensed that one day she would awaken to this aspect of herself and release her ego. The external world had captivated her attention for the time, and she was not ready.

I removed gunk from around the heart as I polished her tarnished star, her unique essence of light. A star is always bright, whole, perfect, and complete beneath discoloration caused by the ego. I cleared around her heart so it could sing the song it was meant to sing. A connection between the heart and the soul makes one feel alive, loved, and excited about what is coming next, even if that is unknown. There is a sense of trust. The soul seeks lasting, deep, abiding peace, contentment, and acceptance for fulfillment. It does not seek an overscheduled calendar of events. I communicated to her the importance of silence and using the breath to ease the body and the mind to align with the heart center while stating gratitude for all her blessings.

The moral of the story is that perfectionism or idealism is an illusion we create, not a true marker of worth. We make it up in our minds. *What is perfect?* we may wonder, and then a chase begins in whatever direction we are pulled to seek the perfection that we just made up in our minds, often losing sight of the essence of why we do what we do. The soul is left in the dust. This separation of effort and wisdom leads to distress, feelings of being less than enough, disappointment, and failure, despite how hard we try.

To heal the heart and hear the call of her soul and her spirit guides, she must develop an appreciation for the soft, quiet voice within to guide her. Silence and reflection are keys to finding the miracles in her life. Our free will and conscious choice aligned with our higher selves will create our reality and destiny. A miracle can come from connecting to her higher self.

Selflessly Powering Through

A morbidly obese gentleman came for a healing energy session to reduce stress and to get his health on track. He told me, "I am in a fast-paced, intense, decision-making career with a stressful relationship with my coworkers, and I care for my wife with a chronic disease. I am responsible for many people. They rely on me at work and at home. I am so pressured. I just show up and power through the best I can. I don't know if I can do it anymore. I need help." He was sweating from walking up one flight of stairs to my healing energy room. He said all his joints hurt. He had the most beautiful blue eyes and a genuine smile when he greeted me. I could see why people liked and trusted him.

I asked him if he had a belief in a higher power. He said, "No, I haven't really thought about it. My mind is constantly on all the tasks I have to do—yes, what I *have* to do, or people will not have what they need. They rely on me." It was clear to me that his choice to help others was made at the cost of his health and well-being.

My energy and intuitive assessment revealed that his mind was scattered, overwhelmed, and not able to prioritize tasks. It was like watching a video of his life. He responded to every request frantically just to get it done and then beat himself up for not being on top of his game. I could see tiny arrows flying at him from every direction. He clearly had no boundaries or sense of self-worth, although it was clear to me that he truly cared for others and wanted to please them.

I asked him if he loved himself. He told me, "I have no concept of what those words mean." Nowhere in his mind could he comprehend loving himself. Seemingly unable to fathom the possibility with a puzzled expression on his face, he asked, "Is it okay to put myself first, to think of me?"

To emphasize the point, I held my open hands in front of myself. I said, "Try to imagine a balanced scale. You are on one side, and the world is on the other side. Each of us must find inner balance, health, and well-being before taking on tasks for others. If you were on a plane crashing, you would put the oxygen mask on yourself first to avoid dying while trying to help someone else." He realized that was exactly what he was doing—killing himself and alienating others with his intensity. He gave himself permission to care for himself first.

He lamented, "What if I do not do everything I am doing, and something does not turn out well for others? I am responsible." The truth was that if he could not put the oxygen mask on himself, he could not help others. And when his health failed, who would run the business or care for his wife? There is support in the universe for him; he is not alone. I was able to clear his foggy mind so that clarity could lead to conscious decision making. He then could prioritize his tasks with love and compassion. Relationships with his colleagues will go better, too, from a state of peace and calm. He had a huge heart and truly cared for others; with a healthy mind and body, he will be able to do more for others too.

I do not think he could stop long enough to consider these simple truths. He was caught up in doing for others and was exhausted. He realized the key to long-term health and well-being was self-care. He was ready to learn the tools to clear his mind so that he could be fully present and make conscious choices in his life. I suggested he frequently pause during his busy day and say to himself this affirmation: "This breath is for me. When I love myself, I make choices that nourish and nurture my body. I choose to love myself."

The moral of the story is that, once in a state of harmony, we will attract more harmony. This client had much work to do to change his habits. He now understands that breaking the cycle of stress intermittently throughout his day gives him a chance to reset his energy system. His unique essence buried beneath responsibility can now shine in the world, one breath, one moment, and one day at a time.

***

A soul incarnating for an earthly experience carries the story of every life ever lived and every experience in the afterlife. Where we are before we incarnate is a mystery to the human mind, the conversation among our soul group unknown; and the lessons and gifts we are intended to embrace is a journey of self-awareness. It is important to slow down and connect deep within your soul to prioritize your choices so that you can achieve what is most important to you and fulfill your soul's purpose.

Summary of an Understanding of Souls between Worlds

Souls are born into an earthly experience and born into the afterlife at death. There is a cycle of life and death that continues.

The major points from this section are as follows:

- You are a divine being of light. You always were and always will be.
- Grief can be a doorway to understanding your true essence and soul's purpose.
  - o Healthy grieving comes in waves and is not constant.
  - o Self-actualization is often prompted by a tragedy, a trauma, or the death of a person.
- Your loved ones are closer than you think.
- There is support for our loved ones in the afterlife.
- A soul seeking an earthly experience will find a birth or adoptive mother.
- Every soul is on its own journey, and we cannot always know their stories or why they leave us.
- You are a soul having an earthly experience.

PART 3
Your Energy Field

The fundamental assumption in understanding your energy field is that you are a unique being of light vibrating at your unique frequency. The universe is a highly organized and structured system of subatomic particles that move within and around your body and your awareness. An understanding of this energy system and its rich laws can give you the tools to live a more meaningful, healthy, abundant life. Do you have an open mind? Can you believe in something that you cannot see with your physical eyes and learn to trust your intuition, heart, and soul? If so, enjoy the teachings I have for you in this section on Your Energy Field.

CHAPTER 11
The Energy Laws and You

You will find insights for your soul journey through an understanding of your unique essence and the energy laws of our highly structured universe. Energy laws are impersonal and affect everyone and everything at all times. The following are some relevant concepts that will provide you with a foundation so that you can apply these laws in your life.

Unique Essence of Light

There is only one you! The sparkle of you is always the sparkle of you. You will ever glow in this life and the afterlife. Fundamentally, you are a flicker of *light*, the unique essence of who you are, who you have always been, and who you always will be. This flicker of light is whole, perfect, and complete at the core of your being. It is you who came into the womb to have an earthly experience with a plan for this lifetime.

Even identical twins contain their own uniqueness, just like a snowflake or a fingerprint. Energy cannot be created or destroyed; it is transformed. What is true about your light is always true. Have you ever thought of a friend or family member who lived miles away, and the next thing you knew they called you on the phone? Each of you identified the unique essence of the other through the ether-net.

The quantum law of constant motion[19]: once in motion, always in motion. Even after death, nothing stops moving. Molecules may dissolve into dust, but the dust continues to flicker into the space around it, beyond

---

[19] Stack Exchange. "State of constant motion," accessed October 3, 2018, retrieved from https://physics.stackexchange.com/questions/106158/state-of-constant-motion.

human sight. Nothing is static; everything is in motion. A pebble dropped into a pond sends ripples through the water, and the ripples reach everyone standing in the pond eventually, no matter how small they become. The stars in the night sky emit a wave that started many years ago and still reaches us.

An atom is 99.9 percent space. The body is more space than matter. According to science, an atom is 99.9 percent space.[20] What is in that space? Could it be consciousness, particles of light, possibilities, magic, or miracles? At the subatomic level, your physical body is no longer solid but a trillion-plus moving particles of light.

The universe is infinite. We are not limited by time and space. The best estimates from astronomers are that there are at least one hundred billion galaxies in the observable universe. The sun is one of about two hundred billion stars (or perhaps more) just in the Milky Way galaxy alone.[21] The vastness of possibilities within the atoms of our bodies and the stars in the universe is beyond reason. There is more that we cannot see than we can see. Light from the most distant galaxy will reach us eventually, and our unique *light* will travel to that infinite galactic universe. As we breathe in subatomic particles from the quantum field, we could breathe in a particle of light from a distant star. We could become part star. In fact, I am sure of it.

Law of interconnectedness[22]: All is one. A drop of water in the ocean is the ocean. A drop of water is not separate from the ocean. A cup of pond water poured it into the ocean would be folded into the ocean and would not be distinguishable from the ocean. We are all one; what affects one affects us all because we share the quantum field. We are never separate from the field.

Law of reaction: Each and every action has an infinite number

---

[20] *Jefferson Lab*, "Questions and Answers," accessed April 22, 2019, retrieved from https://education.jlab.org/qa/how-much-of-an-atom-is-empty-space.html

[21] *NASA*, "Hubble Reveals Observable Universe Contains 10 Times More Galaxies than Previously Thought," last modified August 6, 2017, retrieved from https://www.nasa.gov/feature/goddard/2016/hubble-reveals-observable-universe-contains-10-times-more-galaxies-than-previously-thought

[22] Zoe Blarowski, "How Quantum Physics Bridges Science and Spirituality," *Care2*, April 26, 2018, retrieved from https://www.care2.com/greenliving/how-quantum-physics-bridges-science-and-spirituality.html

of reactions and possibilities. In Newtonian physics, every action has an equal and opposite reaction.[23] In quantum physics, every action has an infinite number of reactions.[24] Every thought, word, and emotion sets in motion an infinite number of reactions. There is no one-to-one correlation between cause and effect because every action can be affected by numerous other reactions. We may never know why some events happen; the possibilities are too complex for us to understand.

Law of gravity: We are connected to Mother Earth. We are literally held to the earth by gravity as a mother holds her child close to her chest and sends love to the child. So does Mother Earth send love to humans, plants, and animals. This energy is right below your feet at every moment, no matter if you are in a plane or on a boat. Even if you live on the hundredth floor of a high-rise, the earth's energy is available to you. The earth is called Mother Earth because her vibration is loving, nurturing, and nourishing. The earth nourishes us.

Law of Attraction: Like Attracts Like

The law of attraction[25] is the idea that whatever we give our attention to will become part of our lives. An energy law that vibration attracts like vibration supports the concept that our thoughts have specific vibrations and will attract similar vibrations.

Our thoughts are powerful tools to attract to us that which we desire. We can attract things that we do not want as easily as we attract things that we want by thinking about them a lot. There are three steps to deliberately attract what you want: clearly identify what you want, focus your thoughts intently, and allow it to manifest in your life.

The conclusion is that all of these laws are in effect at all times for everyone. The human eye cannot see the subtle energy flowing within and around our bodies and environment. An understanding of these energy

---

[23] "Propulsion," accessed April 22, 2019, retrieved from http://www.qrg.northwestern.edu/projects/vss/docs/propulsion/2-every-action-has-an-equal-and-opposite.html

[24] Robert Coolman, "What Is Quantum Mechanics?" *Live Science*, September 26, 2014, retrieved from https://www.livescience.com/33816-quantum-mechanics-explanation.html

[25] Freya Martin, "What Has the Law of Attraction to Do with Quantum Physics?" *Quora*, July 12, 2018, retrieved from https://www.quora.com/What-has-the-Law-Of-Attraction-to-do-with-Quantum-Physics

laws can bring an awareness to the effect of our choices on our lives and teach us tools to manifest, heal, and transform our lives.

An understanding of energy laws can change your perception of events and allow you to heal and fulfill your destiny. There are markers and guideposts within each and every one of us that illuminate our paths. Some are obvious, as when you stumble over twigs in the woods as a gentle nudge from nature to slow you down and invite you to pay attention; a subtle stirring of a soft, quiet voice inside your head; or a forceful reminder that stops you dead in your tracks as though you were hit over the head with a universal two-by-four. There is much beneath the surface of your physical reality.

CHAPTER 12
The Anatomy of Your Energy Field

Everything in the universe is within you. Ask all from yourself.
Rumi

The universe is organized and structured for the success of individuals, our society, the global community, and the intergalactic community, and so is your energy field. The energy flowing beneath the surface of our physical reality is where magic and possibilities reside. These truths reveal how inadequate reality is to account for the inconsistencies that we see, hear, and feel in the world. An understanding of how to collaborate with these laws can shatter your worldview, bring you joy, heal disease, and manifest abundance in an instant.

Your world is perceived by your energy field as it interprets the charge of subtle particles of light that you cannot see. Beyond your five senses, you can feel your emotions, entertain your thoughts, receive intuition, and—for the lucky ones, feel blessed from spirit. The reasoning mind is not enough to explain what you do not understand.

There is so much information available to you through your energy system. An understanding of the effect of these charges on your energy system within and around your body will help you to navigate your nonphysical reality and change it. An understanding of the energy system and the universal laws changed my life, and it can change yours too. It is so exciting to begin to understand that which we cannot see.

Researchers from around the globe mapped energy systems and found strong similarities.[26]

1. The energy centers rotate clockwise to pull in universal life force from the quantum field, creating a vortex of energy into the core of the energy system.
2. Each center vibrates at a specific color, affecting specific endocrine glands and organs of the body, and is developed during different stages of human development.
3. The energy system is mechanical in the sense that we all have the same system.
4. The attributes of the soul journey are aligned with the location of the energy centers on the body.
5. A balanced and clear energy system leads to peace, calm, mental clarity, heightened intuition, an enhanced immune system, and more resilience to life stressors.
6. It is essential to connect your unique essence to the earth and the heavens for vitality.
7. A peaceful state creates optimal health and well-being, nourishes the organs of the body, and resets the endocrine system to avoid overstimulation of the adrenals and subsequent cascade of hormones.

A healthy energy system creates an optimal flow of energy through the body and can lead to an antiaging, antipain, antisad, and antistuck remedy. You can maintain a healthy field by engaging people, places, experiences, and things that enhance a positive flow of energy through your system. Any disruption in the flow of energy in and around your body can lead to physical, mental, emotional, and spiritual dis-ease.

This system of energy that permeates the physical body to support and sustain it is called the etheric body. All life forms including plants and

---

[26] Cyndi Dale, "Chakras Around the World: Are There Really Seven Chakras?" *Llewellyn*, accessed June 10, 2018, retrieved from https://www.llewellyn.com/journal/article/2537

animals have etheric bodies. The etheric[27] body is an energy grid within the energy system and forms a structure of meridians throughout the body. These meridians run through all the major organs, glands, nerves, and energy centers. Nothing can be alive without it because it feeds the physical body with vital life force for health and survival.

Knowledge of the energy system is needed to transform and to maintain a healthy physical, emotional, and mental body. The pathways within the energy system provide information on the vibrancy of the life force coming into the body, where the energy flow is deficient or excessive and creates a focused pathway to resolve issues. This knowledge informs you so that blocked energy can be released, healed, or resolved through healing energy. Once blocks are released, most individuals tell me they feel more like themselves, empowered, hopeful, and loving.

The field around your body is called a biofield or auric field, and it surrounds your physical and etheric body and beyond. This beautiful field of light energy provides a protective cushion for your unique essence of light. Many individuals can see colors in the auric field that represent the frequency of light in the field at that moment in time. The energy you send and receive can be filtered and stored in the biofield.

Have you ever sensed that someone was in your space although they were a few feet away? You were sensing someone in your biofield. Humans can sense and feel one another's charges—for example, anger or love. The charges created in your field are sensed by the subtle energy bodies within your energy system. You know when you meet someone who is in vibrational alignment with you. It feels natural, harmonic, and easy to just be yourself.

Other times you may have met someone with whom you would prefer to have no interaction; you were sensing a discordant charge when reading the charges in their field. You see, you are a multisensory being of light!

Your thoughts, words, and actions emit electromagnetic waves into your energy biofield (auric field) and the environment around you. Theses waves of light either enhance or diminish your life force. Unresolved

---

[27] The etheric body is a body of energy that permeates the physical body, giving it sustenance, health, and vitality, without which the physical body could not be alive. All life forms, including plants and animals, cannot live without the etheric body as it feeds the physical body with energy that is vital for its health and survival.

emotion, trauma, grief, anger, and shame can create a weight and unhealthy trail in the biofield.

Experiences, people, places, and things can cloud your spirit, distract your mind, overwhelm your emotions, and cloud your biofield, which can lead to physical dis-ease. You can create a healthy biofield by clearing and maintaining your field.

Vibrational autonomy is a term that means the vibrations within and around your energy field are in vibrational alignment with your unique essence. In a state of vibrational alignment, you experience peace, calm, mental clarity, and heightened intuition.

Everyone constantly sends and receives information in the form of charges both consciously and subconsciously. The spectrum of a person's ability to receive and send is quite broad. Intuition is an inner source of knowing aligned with universal consciousness. The subtle energy bodies I am speaking about in this chapter have more to do with interpreting the energy field itself than the innate knowledge in your heart and soul.

Receivers can sense the electromagnetic charges of others. Receivers who are in tune with their environment and interpret it correctly can flow better. They self-adjust their tones of voice, gestures, and requests as needed to create harmony.

Receivers can also shut down their ability to sense the charges in the field emotionally, mentally, physically, and spiritually. It can feel like depression, confusion, exhaustion, and even a sense of being lost.

Receivers who are highly sensitive to smells, taste, light, sound, emotion, and thought are often overwhelmed. When unfiltered, this stimulation can lead to migraines, pain, anxiety, panic attacks, uncontrollable weeping, and generalized discomfort.

A hardened field limits the ability to receive light and love. I have seen clients whose biofields were as impenetrable as Plexiglas or steel. People will often say, "I do not feel loved or appreciated." The lack of love in and out of the field leads to resentment and lack of joy.

An overexpanded field is porous to electromagnetic charges and can be overwhelming to an individual. There is too much stimulation to sort out. An empath can have an expanded field and detect the emotions of others in an entire room at the same time. An empath must learn to set healthy boundaries to avoid excessive charges.

An empathic individual is a highly sensitive receiver of electromagnetic waves in his or her environment. Often this acute sensitivity leads to intense reactions to people, situations, or events. And as humans we can turn that intensity towards ourselves, wondering, *What is wrong with me?* If you are empathic, being able to interpret the electromagnetic waves takes practice. You may have heard from someone that you are too sensitive and to "get over yourself." You can prepare for situations that are highly stimulating through a breathing technique; see the appendix.

Senders have a spectrum of abilities that range from intrusive into the energy fields of others to lacking the ability to communicate their emotions, thoughts, or needs. I have worked with people who work so hard at sending energy out that they become incapable of receiving love and appreciation from others.

Senders who are in tune with the energy field can interpret others' responses to the energy they send so that they can modify the intensity of the energy to create more flow. They self-regulate the energy they send consciously.

A client told me about how she had held her sick grandchild in the hospital. She sent love through her hands while holding the baby, and the infant relaxed. She embraced her power to heal. Love heals; send your love to those you love.

For optimal communication, the sender and receiver need to be on the same wavelength to share thoughts and ideas. For example, if you want to watch a specific show on television, you have to select the channel that is playing that show. You cannot just turn on the television and expect your show to be on. You may need to consider the timing and then adjust the volume so you can hear it. The subtle energy bodies work in the same way. Adjust the channel, time, and volume for optimal results.

Imagine today that you are happy, productive, and in your zone. You greet people at the store in a warm and friendly manner, and they respond to your energy kindly. On another day, you enter the store rushed and irritated and resist a kind overture from the cashier. The cashier may sense your lower vibration, respond with disinterest to you, and go through his or her routine in a perfunctory manner so as not to engage you. The universe responds accordingly, drawing to you that which is vibrating at the frequency you are emitting.

The translation of sending and receiving charges is an art and develops over time as you track your interactions. Your heightened awareness of the charges in your field and the fields of others is just the beginning. There is so much more to the invisible world. This is a stepping stone. When you are mindful and fully present in the moment, you are open to your intuition, spirit guides, and more.

You can practice sending and receiving charges. In order to send the energy of appreciation to another, you must raise your frequency to that of appreciation. A simultaneous exchange is a win-win for both of you. Appreciation is a pleasant high-frequency charge to receive.

Another practice you can initiate is to receive a compliment graciously. Someone notices your new outfit and tells you how marvelous you look. You make eye contact, smile, and acknowledge their compliment, and you offer a warm, "Thank you for noticing."

Now imagine someone thanks you for something you did for them. Instead of brushing it off, offer a heartfelt, "My pleasure." You honor someone when you receive appreciation that they send to you.

Appreciation is a frequency of light always available to you from the cosmos. And to your surprise, subtle changes in your life may occur once you set in motion small acts of kindness. This reciprocity of appreciation can change your life.

***

The weight of emotions within your field can be sensed as well. Someone might say, "I feel down" or "I feel low" as though the gravitational pull of the earth has become stronger. They may say, "I feel stuck," as though they are held to the earth and unable to fight the pull of gravity to move forward or in any direction at all. Someone might say, "I feel light" when excited, joyful, or inspired, as though he or she is being lifted toward the heavens.

Our bodies weigh the same, yet our experiences in our bodies are different depending on our states of mind, our thoughts, and our emotions. The gravity of thought and emotions create weight in the biofield. You can shift your thoughts to be more positive to build a healthier field. A healthy field supports you in your effort to be the best you can be.

Every thought has a charge, and repeating the same thought over and over creates a cluster of the same frequency, called a thought form, which can limit the flow of energy through the mind. Energy needs to flow to solve problems successfully. Have you ever said, "I need to clear my head"?

What is in your head? Thought forms? You can choose to let old thoughts out and allow new thoughts in. New ideas or solutions to problems can rise to the surface when you are in vibrational alignment. Just as you clean out your closet once a year, you need to clean out your head and neutralize your emotions.

You can attune to your environment and interpret its effect on your energy field to allow you to make an adjustment in real time. Let us suppose that you entered a room and there was palpable tension among the people there. What would you sense? Here are some possible ways someone might respond.

- A highly sensitive individual with a porous field may soak up the tension in the room and may not be able to detect the source of the tension. They can become overwhelmed and confused. They may talk to whomever they happen to be near. People who are overwhelmed often talk too much or react awkwardly.
- An individual may not be able to detect specific charges due to a rigid field. This person may be guarded and may not be able to discern a vibrational match to have a conversation. People like this may choose to isolate themselves and avoid contact.
- A healthy field does not allow tension to enter the field and can find allies in the room with whom to strike up a meaningful or enjoyable conversation.

Most of us are somewhere on the spectrum depending on the day and can be either too sensitive or too rigid. The point is that no matter what the charge is in the room, you can remain neutral and stand in your vibrational autonomy.

Once you have established your essence of light and filled your field with its vibrancy, you can spread your field out wide and send light into the world. Sister Eleanor Dooley, a Sister of Joseph who taught integrated spirituality at Elms College, had an immense aura of white light though she was less than five feet tall and a hundred pounds. The first time I heard her speak I detected an aura ten feet in diameter. I told myself I would study with her one day. She is a living mystic.

And I did study under her tutorage. She told our class, "When I walked down the streets in India people moved out of my way. They actually cleared the sidewalk for me to pass. I was humbled." Although she did not take up much space, her presence was felt. You have probably met people in your life whose energy was so vibrant that you just wanted to be around them. Of course, you may be the one who attracts the attention of others. If so, keep spreading your light! A healthy energy field ignited with your unique essence is the key to finding your purpose in life and to cast your beacon of light into the world to draw to you that which is yours to have, to do, and to hold.

A healthy biofield is egg-shaped. Our thoughts and emotions create the texture and shape of our biofields and can distort them as well. A contracted field represents a need for protection. The feelings of being vulnerable or powerless can cause people to contract their fields to be as tight as a surfer's wet suit. Every stimulus that touches the body is intensified, like mini electric shocks.

An example of how your mind can shrink your biofield is as follows. Have you ever watched the news in the morning and then not been able to get a traumatic story out of your head? The story in your head can drain your energy system and commandeer the precious resource of your mind. Your mind receives, assimilates, stores, and plays back information that it takes in. After all, that is the job of the mind.

You have a powerful mind, so observe yourself when you attach to stories that are lowering your frequency. Change your thoughts! You can release the emotion or thought before it disrupts your energy field, and you can prepare for the news by raising your frequency before you watch it. An anxious mind and feelings of helplessness cloud the biofield and drain your life force, so be conscious of the energy that you choose to allow into your field.

The result is reinforced vulnerability and more shrinking of the field. People often state, "I do not feel safe. I feel powerless." Attachment to the news in the morning, disasters, politics, and social discord can contract the field. Humans do not have the power to change global and national events in an instant. When you hold a charge of powerlessness, you diminish the life force energy flowing through your body.

A shield of energy protection can be created before watching the news, checking e-mails, attending crowded events, or engaging with negative people so that you can be your compassionate, true self. You can take in information and not the charge triggered by that information.

A lower frequency, such as worry, fear, and disappointment, can build up over time and lead to anxiety, despair, depression, irritability, and lack of passion for life. A higher frequency and a balanced energy system can build resistance to life stressors—the strength to weather any storm when you are in vibrational alignment.

I always think of the roly-poly, round-bottomed, egg-shaped, inflatable clown that toddlers play with. They knock the clown over, and it bounces back up no matter how many times it gets knocked down. The nature of the clown is to be in balance with the center of gravity at its base. It may wobble while seeking balance, but balance it does. Just give it a minute. You can too. Choose your thoughts and emotions wisely.

Hara Line

Hara means "sea of energy," and this is exactly what it is. The etheric envelope is like an infinite ocean of energy. A clear hara is essential for health and vitality. It is the gateway into the higher dimensions of love and light.

While the biofield relates to your emotions and thoughts, the hara corresponds to your life task and your deeper spiritual purpose. The hara line runs through the center of your body and connects to Mother Earth below your feet, your power center below the navel, your heart center, and an individuation point above your heads, connecting you to the cosmos. A disruption in the flow of energy through the hara leads to a feeling of being separate, alone, and lost without a purpose, and the physical body does not thrive.

A connection to the earth through visualization keeps us grounded to its large, electromagnetic power source. Mother Earth vibrates at a frequency of love, healing, and peace, which supports us to function on the physical plane. This connection is essential for humans, plants, and animals.

The hara line should be in vertical alignment with the body from head to toe. This alignment is essential to live with intention, find the soul's true purpose, and bring joy and happiness.

The hara can become skewed. I have seen patients who are undergoing chemotherapy and are literally beside themselves where the hara line is outside the physical body or pulled to the left or the right.

The right side of the body holds the masculine energy of responsibility, tasks, authority, and the physical world's demands. All work and no play can skew to the right. The left side of the body holds the feminine energy of the softer side of life, emotions, and the ability to nurture the self and others. Someone who is overwhelmed by emotions and lack of self-care can skew to the left. All men and women must balance these energies for proper alignment.

An individual can have physical issues on one side of the body, indicating the hara is out of alignment. A right shoulder, right knee, or right ankle wound indicate an uneven focus on tasks and responsibilities. The first thing I do is a hara alignment.

The conclusion is that when you are attuned to your energy field and the electromagnetic charges that you are sending and receiving, you can make course corrections when you are out of alignment. You can find the peace that already exists within your physical, mental, and emotional subtle energy bodies by strengthening and resetting your energy field.

CHAPTER 13
Spinning Wheels of Light

The energy centers have been mapped by indigenous cultures from around the world. The similarities in the ancient teachings are remarkable, universal, and timeless. In the Hindi model from India, the chakra is a spinning wheel of light that receives, assimilates, and releases energy from the body. Knowledge of the subtle energy bodies and energy centers within the body provides a road map to healing.

Spinning wheels of light create a vortex to receive energy from the universal quantum field, which is essential to sustain all life forms on earth, including humans, animals, and plants. When these systems are optimal, we nourish the organs of the body and all anatomical and physiological systems. The flow through the subtle energy bodies within these systems nourishes, heals, and fortifies.

The Hindi model identified seven chakras on the body and five beyond the body. There are twelve layers in the biofield. Each has specific characteristics associated with your soul journey.

Each chakra is associated with a specific type of energy, and if you address your life at the level of each chakra, you can create health and harmony in your life. Posture, open hands, and uncrossed legs are important to the flow of energy as well. The following is a brief explanation of the seven energy centers on the body.

- **Root Chakra:** The first chakra is where we begin our soul journey. The root gives us a foundation, a sense of safety and security in the world. We learn about our world through tribal consciousness. Your core beliefs are reinforced by your tribe. These tribal beliefs can limit self-expression as we individuate. The root chakra invites the light, love, and energy of the earth into the energy body through the feet and perineum. When connected to the earth, we can get things done in the physical realm. We honor our bodies as a temple and develop deep roots before embarking on our spiritual journey.

If the Root Chakra Is Excessive: Individuals are often overweight and have difficulty losing weight, feel stuck, lack a sense of lightness and freedom, become rigid, need to know why, need to control, and need to be right to create safety. Subconsciously, people tend to overeat so that the charge of anger, fear, guilt, and more has someplace to go. They need more mass to absorb the charge often due to fear of the world.

If the Root Chakra Is Deficient: Individuals are often skinny, flighty, have insufficient mass to settle down, and the charge does not have any place to go. Humans are electrical beings and need to be grounded just like the electrical current in the wall outlet. Not being grounded can lead to burnout. We must release excess charge (as with anxiety) from our field though our feet into the ground with the intention to release that which no longer serves us. The characteristics of people who are not grounded are that they cannot find their keys, are late for appointments, are easily scattered, are not able to complete projects, and feel abandoned.

Affirmation for Healing: "I am safe, I honor my body, and I have passion for my life."

Element: Earth

Color: Red

Body Parts: Feet, knees, hips, perineum, and the tail bone

Tool: You can learn to feel safe and secure in your physical body with some simple grounding exercises to anchor yourself and give yourself a firm foundation for your life journey. In order to ground yourself, imagine you are a tree growing roots deep into the earth, walk barefoot, or spend time in nature to connect to the earth.

- **Sacral Chakra:** The second chakra has to do with honoring the self and honoring another in a relationship as two. When you allow emotions to move through your energy body, you flow more with the ebb and flow of life. This chakra is where you create passion for your life by embracing what you enjoy and making sure that life is a pleasant experience. Emotions are messages that draw you toward what feels good and move you away from that which is uncomfortable. Emotions are your navigational system, like the GPS in your car. If the voice says to go a certain way and you decide to do something different, it does not always turn out well. A healthy sacral chakra is able to experience healthy emotions like pleasure, gratitude, intimacy, desire, and passion. These feelings nurture your creative connection to others.

If the Sacral Chakra Is Excessive: Individuals will express too much drama, hysteria, or intensity that is not called for in the moment. Emotions dominate decisions and life experiences and can lead to constipation or loose bowels, urinary problems, and intimacy and reproductive issues.

If the Sacral Chakra Is Deficient: Individuals will seem rigid, have a lack of playfulness, be unable to feel emotions, and not be able to feel the world around them.

Affirmation for Healing: "I trust and allow emotion to move through me. I create close bonds in my relationships."

Element: Water

Color: Orange

Body Parts: Bladder, uterus, ovaries, large intestines, lower abdomen, and back

Tool: You can create flow of emotions out of the body through dance and movement. You can bless the water you drink with a positive intention.

- **Solar Plexus:** The third chakra relates to the digestive organs and is the engine that fills us with vitality, fire, strength of will, and our true power. It helps to steer our lives and gives us the energy to keep going during difficult times. The fire in the belly gives you the power so that you have the will to get things done.

    If the Solar Plexus Chakra Is Excessive: Individuals use their power over others, overthink, overdo, take unreasonable risks, power through situations, and accept too many tasks to feed the ego. The ego runs the show. Anger, resentment, and too much responsibility can lead to issues in the liver, pancreas, and gall bladder.

If the Solar Plexus Chakra Is Deficient: They are not able to make healthy choices due to a lack of personal power, limiting beliefs, feeling like victims, powerlessness, not taking chances in life, and playing it safe. Worry builds in the spleen.

Affirmation for Healing: "I empower myself and others at all times."

Element: Fire

Color: Yellow

Body Parts: Digestive organs, spleen, liver, pancreas, stomach, small intestines, gall bladder, upper abdomen, and midback

Tool: You can pause to make conscious choices; say yes when you mean yes and no when you mean no.

- **Heart Chakra:** The fourth chakra is about the inner journey to discover who you are, what you are, what gifts you have to share with the world, and what you need. The heart integrates the first three chakras of the physical world of what we have, feel, and know; our inner selves; and the three chakras above the heart of the nonphysical world. The heart is the most powerful rhythmic energy field in the body, and as it becomes more organized, we have more power to love ourselves and others.

If the Heart Chakra Is Excessive: Individuals are codependent, overcompensate for the need for love by suffocating others, and are idealist and perfectionist.

If the Heart Chakra Is Deficient: Individuals feel a lack of self-love and self-worth, are critical of themselves and others, lack acceptance, and lack forgiveness. They often self-sabotage.

Affirmation for Healing: "I love myself and others unconditionally."

Element: Air

Color: Green

Body Parts: Heart, shoulders, thymus gland, lungs, upper back, and arms

Tool: This is the chakra where we connect to our breath to find balance and peace. *Spirit* is Latin for "breath." Slow, calm breaths can bring peace to the heart, mind, and body.

- **Throat Chakra:** The fifth chakra is our communication center for self-expression, confidence, creativity, and the ability to speak our truth with grace and ease. The ability to express ourselves and to find freedom from toxic situations is the function of the throat. Sound, as a way to communicate, is important in this chakra; every sound and vibration has an impact on us, and using sound to communicate effectively makes our personal relationships stronger. When you know who you are, you can speak with compassion, grace, and ease.

  If the Throat Chakra Is Excessive: Individuals will talk too much and use harsh words. They do not connect the heart to the voice, and words come out inadvertently.

  If the Throat Chakra Is Deficient: Their voices will be tight and squeaky, and they swallow the truth. They lack confidence, will, and self-expression.

  Affirmation for Healing: "I speak truth with grace and ease."

  Element: Sound

  Color: Sky Blue

  Body Parts: Throat, neck, and thyroid gland

  Tool: You can chant and sing to create movement through the throat chakra. You can write for twenty minutes without stopping or thinking and see where you end up. No editing allowed. You may be surprised. Try it!

- **Brow Chakra:** The sixth chakra is the opening to the third eye, your intuition, imagination, and dreams, where you create a vision for your life. This is the first of the transpersonal chakras, where you start to transcend and detach from your daily life to look at the world from a wider perspective. You could not think, feel, or dream if your mind did not allow old thoughts to die away. You are limited by your five senses to see only the material world, but your intuition senses the nonphysical reality and dissolves the physical world into a bundle of vibrating energy you can see clearly.

  If the Brow Chakra Is Excessive: Individuals receive too much psychic input and cannot discern or sort out their thoughts to see the truth; they experience mental confusion and lack of clarity, and they live in fantasy.

If the Brow Chakra Is Deficient: Individuals see only one point of view and lack vision. They already know the answers and do not need to ask the higher self.

Affirmation for Healing: "I am open to inner wisdom, clarity, and insight."

Element: Ether

Color: Indigo

Body Parts: Brain, eyes, ears, nose, mouth, face, pituitary and pineal glands

Tool: You can embrace the beauty in your world, become curious about your life and your surroundings, open your mind, and see what is before you. You can journal your story.

- **Crown Chakra:** The seventh chakra is where you can expand and raise your consciousness to transcend everything that distracts you in everyday life. The crown connects us to divine wisdom and purpose.

  If the Crown Chakra Is Excessive: Individuals live in the mind, cannot seem to stop thinking, are not able to sleep, and are overly attached to spiritual matters.

  If the Crown Chakra Is Deficient: Individuals lack a spiritual connection, lack a practice to connect with spirit, have feelings of being alone and separate, feel "I have to do this all by myself," and seem lost without purpose.

  Affirmation for Healing: "All is one; trust all is well."

  Element: Thought

  Color: Violet or Purple

  Body Parts: Pituitary and pineal glands

  Tool: You can quiet the mind in meditation. Mindfulness practices can connect you to your higher power and divine wisdom.

Following is a summary of the key attributes of the seven energy centers on the body.

- Root: a sense of being safe and secure
- Sacral: trust your emotions, close bonds in your relationships
- Solar plexus: empower self and others

- Heart: love self and others
- Throat: express truth
- Brow: clarity, insight, and intuition
- Crown: trust, divine wisdom, all is well

These energy centers receive and assimilate subatomic particles from the quantum field and therefore can bring in debris from the environment such as psychic free radicals from the thoughts and emotions of others. A healthy energy center spins clockwise to bring in the universal life force from the quantum field. This spinning can bring with it the psychic free radicals, which can feel like irritability, nervousness, cloudy thinking, and fatigue.

A daily practice of checking in and clearing your energy field from the day-to-day stresses can strengthen your field. You can state gratitude for your blessings to reset and fortify your energy field. It is always easier to clean the slate each day than wait until a major dis-ease expresses itself in your body. Disruptions in the energy system can be detected in your body and your senses.

Do you have an inner knowing deep within the cells of your body that it is time for a change but are not sure what it is? Your body knows before you do; it creates signals of discomfort. Sometimes the universe creates barriers or challenges where there once was smooth sailing. Either way, how can you discern your next steps? The good news is there are processes that can guide you. We all have free will, so it is up to you to take action and to be willing to explore the limitless possibilities. The first step is a balanced energy system.

Imbalance in your energy system leads to physical dis-ease, anxiety, irritation, depression, mental confusion, and lack of connectedness to others. An imbalance presents in many ways, and you know when it is happening or has happened. Do you have an imbalance in your life? How does it present? Are you unable to feel love, ease, or contentment? Or do you feel alone, abandoned, or anxious or exhibit physical, emotional, or mental ailments? Do you lack direction, meaning, purpose, inner guidance, success, close bonds in relationships, or impulse control? All these disruptions in your energy body can be alleviated.

Ancient Global Truth

As early as 1820 BC, Ancient Egyptians documented healing techniques.[28] Ancient tribes and villages such as the Lakota[29] designated a man or woman for healing. They trusted their intuition, their connection to the earth and the heavens, spirits from the invisible world, and the magical power of the human heart. Many cultures beat drums to mimic the heartbeat to calm or excite heart magic.

Have you ever banged your elbow? What happened next? Did you create thoughts in your mind such as, *Ouch! I banged my elbow. What resources do I have readily available to me to relieve the pain? Oh, I have dozens of energy centers in my hands that can enhance the flow of energy to relieve the pain?* Or did you just grab your elbow with your hand and say, "Ouch"?

A mother kisses a child's boo-boo and it feels better. A loved one gently embraces a friend and offers comfort through touch. Our instincts to touch demonstrate our innate knowing that energy flows through our hands to heal. Who knows what level of ability lies inside of you until you explore your innate wisdom to heal? Are you curious about this ability in you?

Try this: open and close your hands several times, clap them together, or rub them until you feel a warm, tingling sensation. Move your hands slowly back and forth facing each other. Do you feel any sensation—a magnetism, polarity, or energetic taffy? You have just awoken the energy centers in your hands to send and receive electromagnetic waves. As humans, we are innately wired to heal ourselves and others through touch. Everyone can drink a glass of wine, but not everyone can taste the essence of an expensive bottle of wine. Practice refines our skills.

Once you have awoken the energy centers in your hands, place them on an area of your body that needs healing as you imagine the energy

---

[28] Rosalie David, "The Art of Healing in Ancient Egypt: A Scientific Reappraisal," *The Lancet* 372 (9652), November 22, 2008, retrieved from https://www.thelancet.com/journals/lancet/article/PIIS0140-6736(08)61749-3/fulltext

[29] Suzanne J. Crawford and Dennis F. Kelley, *American Indian Religious Traditions: An Encyclopedia,* Volume 2, ABC-CLIO; illustrated edition (Santa Barbara, CA: ABC-CLIO, Inc, 2005).

flowing through your hands. The flow of energy is what heals. You can try it on someone else who is willing to explore the possibilities.

If you know someone who is experiencing hospice or palliative care or is postsurgery, you can hold his or her feet and observe the expression on his or her face soften with your loving touch. Any touch with the intent of love can only bring love and end in love. Love does not get transmuted by the universe; it holds as you hold the intention in your mind to send love. I invite you to explore and strengthen your unique abilities to heal. Trust yourself. You have the power within you.

As you gain confidence through your own experience, use your mind's eye to connect with someone who is not with you and send love to them. Focused intention guides your energy to connect to the unique vibration and energy field of the individual you want to receive light and love for healing. The word *love* is a high frequency that can help to shed low vibrations in the field of another. Trust the power of your intention.

To heal means "to make whole," which includes the physical, emotional, mental, and spiritual bodies of the energy system. The power of the mind and the ability to hold a high vibration of love in concert with the energy field is the key to healing yourself and others. Distance healing is possible because of an energetic connection, intention, and love of the sender to the receiver. You do this every day when thinking of someone you love. Now, I want you to really trust that you are making a difference when you send healing to yourself and others. You have power—the power of love.

Religious people use prayer and positive thinking to invite healing for people who are not geographically present. Considerable evidence underscores its effectiveness. Have you ever experienced a change in event or outcome from prayer alone? Or have you had a feeling that something was wrong with a friend or loved one and later found out that you were right?

This phenomenon can be explained by energetic connectivity, which assumes the presence of fields that can generate connections through what has been called a nonlocal reality. All human beings have a sixth sense that transcends time and space. We are connected in a nonlocal reality. Through intention and our energy fields, we interact and communicate information. Quantum physics and subtle energy medicine provide us with evidence on how this transfer of energy, thought, and healing happens.

Feedback from my clients supports that distance healing is just as effective as an in-person session.

A barrier to peace can be eliminated simply by learning processes to clear and balance your energy system and to release stuck, unhealthy emotions and thoughts from your energy field. To maintain your energy system, you need to create healthy boundaries, reset your belief system, and embrace the spiritual truths of the ancients that are still true today. A daily spiritual practice is key. See the appendix for a daily exercise.

CHAPTER 14
The Magic within Your Body

The magic within your body to become you is ignited by your inner light. It is the source of your power to heal, manifest, and live a joyful life. The key is to align your source of power with an understanding of the subtle energy bodies that are vibrating and emitting electromagnetic waves within and around your body.

A clear energy field allows for clear communication and flow in life. Here are some simple ways to enhance and protect your energy field.

- **Be neutral.** You can keep your focus on something positive when another person says something negative to neutralize the charge. Remember to keep in your mind a thought that makes you happy. Simply nod in acknowledgment that you heard the other person. When you defend yourself with emotion, it attaches to the frequency of the energy you are resisting.

  You can always be neutral in your thoughts, emotions, and body language. You know yourself better than anyone. Why would you take someone's words personally? Remain impersonal. One of my practices is that I imagine my body is made up of subatomic particles, and I become invisible as I allow the charge to float through me.

- **Transform energy and try magic on people who complain.** This is a great time to try some magic. You can use your mind's intention to transform energy into a higher frequency. When you begin to sense an uncomfortable charge in the form of a thought, emotion, or word, consciously imagine it turning into a butterfly, a sparkle, a pink cotton ball, or anything you like. Energy is in constant motion; even low-frequency thoughts are moving, so you can move them. The truth is that energy is not good or bad, just different. Do not attach judgment to the people you may perceive as negative. It is your perception. You can transform energy and send it on its way to keep your energy field clear. You can try to shift the frequency with soft music, calming colors, and aromatherapy to subtly raise the vibration of a room where someone is sick, sad, or lonely.

- **Believe peace exists within your heart.** You can step it up a notch and send positive states of awareness to others, such as love, gratitude, compassion, appreciation, and awe of that which stirs your soul.

  Over time your higher vibrational state may help the negative person. You can consider that others really want to be in higher state of awareness and you can help. People who are miserable can adopt a new habit over time. They may lack conscious awareness of the energy they are sending. It is not always a conscious choice. The more someone is in a low vibration, the lower it seems to go. Like attracts like.

  You can help others by changing the charge you are sending to the environment. For a negative person to shift to peace and happiness is not an easy thing to do. It takes time and commitment to want to be in a different state. The key is believing that peace and happiness are possible for everyone. You may be the light that makes a difference to someone. Shine your light!

- **Embrace emotions.** Emotions are navigational tools you can use to learn about yourself. The emotional charge is information in response to people, places, events, and things. The charge of an emotion coming up in you creates an awareness of that which is inside of you.

  For example, when you observe that your nerves are frayed and you are irritable with loved ones, it may be a gentle self-care alert to embrace you for being you. Sometimes a charge can snap our consciousness back into the awareness of what is truly important, especially when the ego is running the show. The emotions that you sense are a sign of your unique human essence. This information can remind you to love yourself more and to manage your choices wisely.

When the energy around you is swirling and twirling, you can shift your thoughts to imagine a never-ending celebration of life, a dance the universe is dancing and inviting you to dance too. Dance and enjoy the tapestry of your life. Although your life may appear chaotic, trust the universe has designed every detail of a much bigger operation.

Somedays you can shift your mind to trust and somedays you cannot. Love yourself on both days and know the constant motion of the universe will move you forward. The more you practice this shift in thinking with the small stuff, the more you build your personal power to handle the bigger stuff. Practice and you will see signs of improvement.

- **Negative people.** How should you be with negative people? You must focus on what is truly positive in your life and not allow your attention to sink to their lower vibration. Eventually, by keeping your vibration high, you will affect the vibration of the person who is emitting a lower one. I had a client who was concerned that she attracted the negative people in her office. When I asked her to describe her interaction with others during her day, she shared with me that she focused on her work and did not engage others. She was there to earn a paycheck. She never said good morning to her coworkers or asked about their weekends. She did not want to waste time in idol chitchat. She got what she put out.

  People perceived that she did not like her colleagues, and she attracted others who were disengaged at work. Like attracts like. A simple change to saying good morning and make eye contact without the fear that her time would be wasted led to feeling more like she belonged with her peers. She found that she was included in activities that led to better teamwork, and she learned from them too. Cooperation and engagement are a win-win!

The following stories demonstrate how you can change the charge in your field and change your life.

Sofia Binged on Poor Food Choices after Her Commute

Sofia was a happy, successful woman who was physically active with strong knowledge of nutrition. She said, "I love my wonderful husband and children. I am lucky. I have a good life, I had a wonderful childhood, and I have no complaints. Life is good. The problem is my weight; I gained ten pounds." Although looking at her, it was hard to understand where she had gained them. She had recently accepted a promotion with recognition and a financial reward. She loved her work and considers it a vocation. But her stress during and after her commute was interfering with healthy food choices, and she was seeking release from that stress so that she and her family could get back on track.

Sofia's commute to and from work was a boring grind with traffic patterns that infringed on her time schedule. She picked her children up from school after work, when they were all tired, hungry, and irritable. A charge formed in her field when she was at the mercy of honking horns and rude drivers. Day after day of the same experience was wearing her down. The first thing Sofia would do when she got home was binge on chips or sweets, or she would stop for fast food for herself and her children.

During the healing energy session, I received messages for Sofia from spirit:

- The decision to choose employment that requires a commute was made with full conscious choice and awareness to fulfill her professional aspirations and share her gifts. She was recognized for her contributions both financially and professionally.
- The children's schools and activities were also chosen with full conscious awareness.
- The time spent in the commute with children could be managed differently.

I worked with Sofia to come up with some new beliefs:

- My career is perfect for me. I love my career, home, and community, and it requires a commute.

- I have no power to change the traffic pattern. I can only change my reaction to the traffic and be a role model for my children, who ride in the back seat of my SUV.
- I consciously breathe slowly and calmly and accept this is the flow of my commute.
- I remember that we are all one. I fill my heart with light and love so that I can spread energy to the others stuck in traffic.
- I choose healthy food to nourish my body and my children's bodies.

Can you think about your day and examine your core beliefs? Can you ascend above the physical plane where the people, places, or experiences send an uncomfortable charge through your energy system to embrace your unique essence from a higher perspective? Sofia did just that. Once she could be neutral to the charge, she could change her reaction and make healthy food choices.

A Charged Conversation

A woman devoted to her spiritual practice came to me for a healing energy session because she was experiencing anger and could not calm her emotions. An unfortunate misunderstanding had occurred and had a ripple effect on her family. Once the energetic charge of anger was ignited, no words of compassion could be heard. An old adage is that when two people are on different wavelengths, no explanation is possible; but when they're on the same wavelength, no explanation is needed.

Prior to the altercation, core beliefs were being challenged. The mother was thinking, *How could my daughter make such a lifestyle choice? She will never have children or financial success if she chooses this vocation.* The mother was worried about her daughter's happiness, and that led to their charged conversations. She could not help interjecting her concerns.

The daughter felt unheard and unsupported by her mother. Her deep desire to explore her vocation and her perception of being threatened by those who challenged her interests set the stage for an inner battle with conflicting emotions, thoughts, and desires. The daughter believed that most people would not understand her choice but acquiesced to her mother's insistence for her to meet with a life coach.

The charges from the emotions within the mother, the daughter, and their relationship were close to the surface. The mother's anger was unleashed on the life coach, who asked thought-provoking questions to her daughter such as, "Are you aware of the long-term commitments you are making? The expectations of this vocation include many rules and obligations. Are you familiar with them? Have you visited and met other initiates to better learn about the vocation?"

The daughter exploded. As a charge built up in her system, she vented at her mom. She said, "I knew it would happen! No one believes I know what I am doing."

This situation was so charged with emotion, it is no surprise anger prevailed. Indignant, the mother asked, "How could anyone be so careless and ask those questions, disrespecting my daughter? How dare you?" The mother could not contain herself. This fully charged event was doomed to happen. The anger and the charge intensified as the story was told and retold to anyone who would listen. The mother defended her position, believing the injustice to her daughter.

By clearing the mother's energy field and neutralizing the charges, she was able to see clearly. Her own fears had been misplaced on the life coach, who had not meant to disrespect her.

The moral of the story is that the mother had been on a spiritual journey for decades, meditating and studying mystical laws, but when it came to her daughter's feeling disrespected, she became a mama bear. So I really only had to remind her of what she already knew. The life coach did not intend for the daughter to feel like the subject of an inquisition.

Sometimes we create our own challenges with our thoughts. The miracle is seeing beyond our emotions and seeing the truth that we are all one. We need one another on this life journey. Ask a friend for help, be a friend, and be kind to yourself when you act emotionally toward others. You can apologize and pay it forward. We are all one.

***

You may be able to think of a time when you became charged by a conversation and then told your partner all about it when you got home.

But the charge was so uncomfortable, all your partner wanted to do was run out of the room. How do you handle the charges that come to your awareness? Do you stop to realize the root of the charge or consider whether you had some clearing to do in regard to a situation? Do you quiet your mind and emotions through a gentle breath? Breathe in peace and calm and breathe out a gentle breath of anger. Once you are in a state of calm, reconsider the situation from a new perspective.

You can imagine that you could place your anger in a cup. You could pour the anger into the ocean and fold it back into the oneness of the ocean. The water in the ocean in not separate from the ocean. The water becomes the ocean, and the ocean is the water. There is no separation. Anger is energy—never good or bad, only different frequencies that dissolve into the wholeness. Anger is only a charge and is moving, so we can move it out.

***

A repetitive charge sent between two individuals in a relationship creates an energy cord. Thoughts, emotions, and charges travel on these cords. Connections to parents, siblings, partners, and friends can be healthy or harmful. Every thought specific to another person either dissolves or strengthens this cord. Have you heard the term *cut the cord* in regard to your children? Parents' cords to their children can keep the children from being empowered. You can have a cord to an ancestor, an event, a person, a place, or a thing. Cords transcend time and space on the earthly plane and into the afterlife.

An angry, divorced couple or children estranged from their parents may want to cut the cord. As long as a charged cord is in place, it can be triggered by events in which you lose your power. If you have ever overreacted to a situation and could not figure out why, you may have a charged cord.

A cord charged with emotions can be triggered and actually recreate an event energetically as though it were happening today. You need to remove unhealthy cords to heal and avoid the triggers of anger.

Other charges in the form of spells are cast with our thoughts, words, and actions and have charges that either enhance or diminish our life force. Thoughts repeated over and over can become a spell that is difficult to break.

You may say to yourself, *I want to stop this behavior, thought, or reaction.* But you just cannot help yourself. This is a form of casting a spell on yourself. A low frequency attracts more of the same low frequency, compounding the spell. You create your own obsession through your thoughts. You recognize a spell when you cannot stop doing, thinking, or saying something that is harmful. An unwanted charge in your field requires focused intention, discipline, and patience to clear. It is not always easy to break a spell.

Worry is an example of a spell. We all know that worry does not solve, relieve, or make problems go away, but that does not stop our minds from repeating scenarios over and over in our heads. Spell casting is not a random thought; it is a focused intention with full, conscious awareness and a specific, desired result. The desired result is not always pleasant; we just cannot stop.

For example, a mother could not stop thinking about her daughter's obsession with her new husband's family. The mother felt ostracized and less important because her daughter spent holidays with the new family. This repetitive thinking was making her sick to her stomach. She had aches and pains in her body and fatigue, but she would not let it go. The mother's desire to change her daughter's behavior was a spell she put on herself but would not reap the desired outcome.

It is the same process to cast a spell on another person. You send your thoughts to another individual. For centuries, witches cast spells through the process of focused attention and intention to transform people, places, and things. Gypsies cast spells on families that lasted for generations. The work of the spell caster occurs in the subtle energy bodies and may not be detected easily.

Spell casters can also provide a person with a positive image or visualization, planting seeds of hope and confidence to achieve dreams. Spell casters can help you to focus on what is good in a person, place, or experience and eclipse the negative, as well as help you see the negative in someone and eclipse the good. In cases of obsession, casting a spell limits the ability to see all the possibilities. In other words, people see what they want to see when under a spell.

Everything is energy, and energy is moving and has its own electromagnetic charge. Thoughts, emotions, and words create charges that can build up and become a spell. Spells are electromagnetic charges in our energy body created by ourselves or others who hold us in a pattern of thought or actions that would normally go against our nature. Spell casters truly exist. In fact, we all cast spells whether we know it or not. Repeated spells can become an obsession to needing something or someone that your rational mind would avoid. People can sabotage themselves with repetitive thoughts that they cannot get out of your heads. It could be a spell you cast on yourself.

Some of the most common spells are when people fall in love, and all they can see is the good in their lovers, ignoring their quirks and challenges. Or think of students who set their sights on certain jobs after graduate school and see no other possibilities. They convince themselves that there is only one perfect job out there.

There are a few ways to protect yourself from a spell.

- Identify when you might be under a spell and consciously choose to release the spell.
- Keep your frequency high to avoid spells.
- You can sense a spell coming your way if you are driven to do something that does not fit your character and you cannot get it out of your head. You can neutralize it by changing your thoughts (or use a magic wand and just imagine—*poof*—it is gone. Remember, it is only energy).
- Observe where you might need to change your pattern of thinking that is not really working and break the spells in your life.
- A healthy relationship with yourself and others creates a flow in your life.

***

There is more than meets the eye. My ability to send and receive charges evolved through conscious intention, effort, and practice so that I can perceive beyond physical reality. I discovered that there is something less tangible behind physical objects, people, experiences, and feelings yet more significant than anything we can see. Are you curious about your life? Then pause, listen, breathe and be fully present in each moment. You can expand your conscious awareness and notice the charges you send and receive, especially those that do harm to yourself or others. You can choose to use your magic wisely!

You can consciously choose to ignite your innate wisdom to see, sense, and feel your environment and discern what is true for you. Are there beliefs you could change or thoughts you could halt as you assess the rhythms in your life for healthy patterns? A conscious assessment of your life and your beliefs in quiet reflection allows you an opportunity to see yourself and those with whom you share your life clearly.

It is time to clear your energy system, be neutral in your emotions, avoid judgment, transform energy with your mind, believe in the possibilities, neutralize spells, and trust your intuition. It may be time to make conscious choices to align with the power within you—your own unique essence of light vibrating at the frequency of you. *You* are the only you there is.

CHAPTER 15
A Soft, Gentle Armor

A soft, gentle armor of love and light within and around your body softens your responses to trials and tribulations. It allows you to respond from a balanced, loving place within your heart. All troubling experiences can be softened with an armor of light and love. Love yourself by knowing who you are, what you need, and the gifts you share with the world. The process is to surrender your ego and live in the higher vibrations. The power of love can be shared with everyone you meet. Most of us struggle to be in this state of harmony. Here are some ideas on how to build your armor.

You are a being of light that has the innate ability to rise above and beyond your physical reality to where there is no body, no mind, no time, and no space. Can you imagine that you are mist? The following is an experience I had while meditating. I became mist.

***

During a group podcast meditation with Danielle Rama Hoffman who channeled Thoth,[30] I envisioned my physical body dissolving as I entered a dreamlike state. Not being in my physical body was freeing. In this blissful state, I became mindfully curious about the essence of the air within and around my body. This sense of bliss happens every time I

---

[30] Joshua J. Mark, "Thoth," *Ancient History Encyclopedia, July 26, 2016,* retrieved from https://www.ancient.eu/Thoth. Thoth is the Egyptian god of writing, magic, wisdom, and the moon. He was one of the most important gods of ancient Egypt. Accessed September 3, 2018.

meditate with this wonderful group of experienced meditators. Our energy together creates an entrainment, amplifying my experience.

In a trance-like state, aligned with Thoth as my teacher, I was invited to witness a mystical experience. I welcomed the invitation. Gently touching my heart with my hand, I became aware of a blissful white light traveling through my chest, down my arms, down my legs, and deep into the earth, all the way to the core of Mother Earth's rich, nurturing womb of healing, love, and light. The white light cleared my energy field until all that was left in my being was pure, white light. I was a light being once again—my favorite state of existence. From there I could travel through the world and see everything from the vantage point of light. My spirit was energized and alive. I wanted to be everywhere and see everything from this sense of being.

Thoth directed me, "Slow down and connect your frequency to nature first. Start with the plants, then move on to the mountains, the oceans, and the seas that vibrate at your frequency to receive their wisdom, welcome, and good wishes."

My internal navigation system located brilliant lights in the vastness of earth. I was drawn to the lights whose frequencies aligned with mine. I recognized that the frequency I was experiencing was that of love, comfort, safety, expansion, and bliss. Thoth reminded me that the world is full of these vibrations of love. It is up to me to find them. Like attracted like vibration. It felt like I was being drawn and light was attracted to me. Any object that came into my vision that was not at my frequency of light disappeared into the horizon. From this vantage point I could sense joy, pleasure, and love in the world.

The joy I sensed when united with these like frequencies ignited an exuberant pulse within me. I had visions of plants common to the Northeast and then unfamiliar plants from around the world. Nature was connected to me around the earth. In the presence of these plants in my mind's eye, the physical form of each plant dissolved into its light frequency when I touched it with my light. We became one in light. I was light, and everything I touched was light. Although I was in the vision, I was also witnessing the light communicating with light. Light communication is a vibration without words. We became one vibrating frequency of light undiscernible from one another. Our combined light ignited us all; neither took from the other, and all was enhanced. I was reminded by Thoth, "All is one and we are all."

Messages from earth highlighted to me that earth has so much to offer humans and is always available. We do not need to strive beyond the earth to find peace and joy. Nature will share it with us. The experience in nature filled my biofield with its vibrant life force, becoming my own protective cushion as I floated toward my family, colleagues, and friends and beyond to those I do not know. I noticed as I floated through my life that my energy affected everyone I met. I felt love for everyone, everywhere.

In my vision, my light body effectively worked like a magic bubble of light that zapped low frequencies of doubt, worry, and fear from people, places, and things that I touched. It was magical! Everything was filled with white light to heal and spread joy to earthly beings.

My biofield became a protective cushion, keeping me safe from external stimuli and allowing me to be in my flow wherever I was and whomever I was with. In this vibration I could be more in the moment and playful. I noticed my grandchildren were more in the flow just because I was in the flow.

I could see the light in and around people as they turned to light too. In a blissful fluid state of nonattachment to the earth, people, places, and things, all things on earth became light—no longer physical forms, simply vibrating frequencies of light.

All forms in nature and the people dissolved. Once again, our light melded together as I floated past the clouds and sky into a galaxy of stars. I could see the earth glow brightly from the heavens. Mother Earth smiled and thanked me for connecting the beauty of the earth with the divine light of individuals, creating a glow around the earth. Our earth star shined brighter with an enhanced, soft, gentle armor of love.

My body felt clear and energized as I returned to a conscious state. My body responded to the white light flowing through me and the poignant message that to be in the flow of my life will bring light and love to our world. I expected to find light, and I found it everywhere I traveled. I had no expectations or doubt that the light energy of love existed. We can create more light for all by being in our flow.

***

During a cloudy, dreary week of torrential rain, wind, cold, and a lunar eclipse, my light body felt dark and heavy. On break at work, I received a call that a dear friend, Margie, was being taken off life support after an unexpected heart attack and sepsis postsurgery. I held back my sobs as I prepared for my next client. I went to get a drink of water to help me swallow my grief and compose myself.

Just then a coworker came out of her office. As she peered through the window, she exclaimed, "I know there is a rainbow out there somewhere! There has to be after so much rain. Look—there is a tiny streak of blue sky popping through." She encouraged me to see through the condensation and rain drops on the window. I squinted and struggled with my tear-filled eyes. It took a little bit to see the narrow blue streak between the dark clouds; the rain had paused in this moment. The blue sky was popping through; I could see it. There was hope for a rainbow. As I allowed myself to be in the moment staring out the window, I felt a deep release of pain from my heart. I sensed my friend's relief that the timing was right for her to leave the earth. It was okay.

We are truly meant to be here for one another in ways you may not understand in advance of an interaction. You never know when a few words of kindness will change someone's day. You can say something nice about the world, the beauty of nature, people, and the unexpected miracles that happen every day. When you share the miracles that come into your life, it will brighten your day and someone else's too. This builds your soft, gentle armor filled with light and love.

Your perceptions can affect how you feel. My mother, who was healing from her second bout of cancer, was under surveillance for an unusual growth at the surgical site. Until the biopsy results came back as normal tissue, she was sluggish, fatigued, and scared of dying, more surgery, and treatments that had almost killed her. Her fear was overwhelming. Once she heard the good news, she became happy, energized, and at peace. The same body now felt light as a feather—proof that her fear was a weight in her energy body, depleting her life force. The unique essence of light was always there. The joy for life was always there. Soon, my father bought a new car. My mother could not wait to show me how easy it was to get in and out of and how she was more comfortable while riding in the car. She acted like a kid at eighty-nine years old.

Fear is a frequency that saps life force, but remember—it is moving, so we can move it out. When you observe your fears, you can make a conscious choice to choose love. You can choose your thoughts wisely to build your life force. You can act more like a kid sometimes; be carefree and accept that what will come will come, especially those things that are out of your control. Why lose life force? You build your armor with your thoughts and beliefs.

Where can you be more in the flow? What do you notice in your world beyond the physical reality? Who and what builds your light? Where do you express and share your light with others? How do you speak to others with light? If you notice a family picture on your coworker's desk, would you ask about it? Have a heart-to-heart conversation with someone you come in contact with randomly during the day. A random act of kindness to share your light with a stranger or colleague can change your life.

The conclusion is that we all know people who are skeptical about life. They usually see what may go wrong and think the worst. You can keep an open mind that today may be the day that you reach them. Today may be the moment they see clearly; do not block the possibilities with your mind. Never give up on those you love because they can surprise you. When you are in the flow, you bring more flow to each interaction and can ask beings of light to assist you too. You can feel free to speak your truths with grace and ease. You do not always have to tiptoe around or sugarcoat your messages. When you mean what you say, you mean what you say. Choose your words wisely and speak from your heart. Your truth, grace, and kindness are your soft, gentle armor.

Following are some tips to build your armor of light.

- Breathe in universal love.
- Keep an open mind.
- Notice beauty in people, nature, and the world.
- Bless your body and bless your life.
- Pray to specific angels or spirit guides for guidance.
- Shine your light, attract light, spread light, and build more light in the world.
- Remember that you are a light being having an earthly experience, so lighten up!

The Summary of Your Energy Field

This chapter addressed an understanding of your energy field, the rich universal laws, and tools to embrace your life with the confidence needed.

You now know the concepts behind the tools that I teach, so you can be an empowered being of light having a rich human experience on your soul's journey toward the afterlife and rebirth of your soul. The practice of implementing these tools takes patience, courage, perseverance, and a loving attitude toward yourself and others. Most of all, lighten up, enjoy your experience, and love your life.

Here are the key points from "Your Energy Field":

- You are a unique being of light.
- You send and receive electromagnetic charges at all times.
- You can create a healthy biofield as your protective cushion from psychic free radicals and low frequencies.
- The laws of our highly structured universe affect all of us, all the time, and are impersonal.

As you anticipate the joy coming into your life with an open mind and heart, you may be surprised at how easy it is to embrace your life. You are developing your intuition, your connection to spirit guides and loved ones. You are not alone. You have much support and knowledge of the nonphysical reality. It is time to envision the future that you want to manifest.

PART 4
On Living a Healthy Life

"There are only two ways to live your life.
One is as though nothing is a miracle.
The other is as though everything is a miracle."
— Albert Einstein

CHAPTER 16
On Beliefs for Healing

Some people plan, sacrifice, and pray and still do not have the lives they hoped for. Unforeseen circumstances appear out of the blue, and their responses to those life events are recorded in their energy bodies. Change is inevitable, and how we handle change is the key. Your beliefs and perceptions of your life experiences can affect how you respond to people, places, and things in your life. Sometimes individuals can be swept forward in their lives by pressures from their families, communities, colleagues, and religious organizations only to find out they are not living the lives they want. You can change your energy body and heal from within; you have the power.

Where did your beliefs come from? Some are forgotten words from your parents, friends, family members, or colleagues who influenced and shaped who you are. All this intermingled with your experiences, knowledge, cultural influences, and even your gender and age can affect how you see yourself and the world.

Other beliefs have been emblazoned on your soul, leaving deep wounds. A failed relationship due to infidelity may lead to a fear of being unworthy or to a lack of the ability to trust the faithfulness of a new partner. A poor choice can lead to berating yourself for being stupid, leading to a lack of self-confidence. These imprints are in your energy field along with all the imprints where you excelled above your family and peers.

The fear of a lack of money may have come when your parents argued over money because money was tight. At the time, the fear of lack was real and there was not enough money to pay the bills. Do you worry about not having enough money? Did you observe marital relationships that were tense and in which harsh words were spouted with little thought of how they landed on a child's senses? How did you receive messages about how you fit in the world as a child? Were words shared with love and kindness, or were your parents' tones harsh and critical? Recall the poem from the seventies: Children Learn What They Live.[31]

How you were raised is not your fault or your parents'. I believe we all do the best we can at each moment in time and that life is our teacher. There is no one to blame; it just is. As humans, we cannot change physical reality, only the invisible trail of its effects. You are no longer a child, so live your life based on what is true for you today.

Early influences in your life affect your beliefs. What if you were chubby as a child and children made fun of you and did not invite you to their birthday parties? You disliked yourself because others disliked you. As an adult, you still carry extra weight and fear others will not like you. This is a limiting belief. Love yourself, love your body, send your bright light into your environment, and others will respond to you. They will see your light. The truth is that we are all different, and the difference in you is what makes all the difference.

The roots of your beliefs are part of your story, but are they true today? Start to notice where and when you sense tension. Is there an outdated belief that you can consciously choose to release? Your life experiences may be embedded in your energy field. You get to choose how to interpret, release, feed, and create beliefs to enhance your self-worth and to build courage. Be conscious of your beliefs, and then create new beliefs that are true for you now.

In a state of peace and calm with guidance and support, you can find a way out of a rabbit hole you crawled down while chasing life. It is a time to peel the layers of the onion away and to connect to the real you.

The truth is that when we know our true selves, we express our true selves with grace and ease, others see us as we truly are, we attract individuals and experiences aligned with our nature, and we find peace and happiness. Mahatma Gandhi said, "Our beliefs lead to our thoughts, our thoughts lead to our words, our words lead to our actions, our actions lead to our behaviors, our behaviors create our destiny."

Many of the clients who come for a healing energy session are blessed

---

[31] Dorothy Law Nolte, "Children Learn What They Live," 1972/1975. See appendix.

in so many ways and yet focus on old perceptions and beliefs that drain their life energy. It is important to live in the present and bless your life. You may find yourself in one of the stories that follow, and you too can give yourself permission to love yourself more and to let go of that which you cannot change.

Abandoned by her Mother

Marie, a poised, well-appointed woman, entered my healing energy room with a smile on her face, her head held high, and a determined look on her face. She displayed a confident demeanor as she described her life as balanced with a happy family, financial success, and national recognition in her field. She was a strong-willed, successful, independent woman whose career had helped thousands of people. She stated, "My friends suggested I try a session with you to balance my energy, I have a very busy life and just want to relax."

In order to get the energy flowing for the healing energy session, I shared my intuitive assessment. I said, "You have so much, yet I sense there is a deep sadness." She looked puzzled, so I clarified for her. "I can see the congestion and blocks in your energy field."

She allowed unrestrained tears to flow from her soft eyes as she described her mother leaving her family when she was young. Through sobs, she shared her story. "What would my life have been like if my mother did not leave? My older sister had to take care of me. I could not do everything other kids got to do with their moms. I did not have a normal childhood." She then described her mother. "My mother has a mental illness and limited ability to care for our family. She became overwhelmed, frustrated, and left all of us and then suddenly returned when I was a teenager." As an adult several decades later, she was still angry and could not accept her mother in her life. She said, "I want nothing to do with her. She didn't want us then; I don't want her now."

I interpreted several messages for Marie from my intuition:

- Her career helped tens of thousands of people.
- Many paths, many choices: if your life had been different, maybe you would not have ended up where you did.

- Your mother did the best she could with her limitations. Accept her as she is.

- Free yourself and cut the cord to your illusion of what childhood should have been. You created a version of a perfect childhood and envied your friends, although you had no idea of their true stories. You made it up. You really did not know what went on in your friends' homes.

- See your mother through the eyes of an adult. The child is no longer a child, and the adult is not abandoned. All is well.

- There are seasons and reasons for people to be in our lives. You can make a conscious choice to include her or not. All is well.

The energy assessment revealed that her heart and throat chakras were compromised and the pain of abandonment lay deep in the tissues of her body. She agreed to release the discordant energy created as a child. New beliefs needed to be activated due to unhealthy neural pathways created by repeating unhealthy beliefs and thoughts.

I recommended that she create a mantra to say when a thought or emotion connected to her childhood came to mind and to replace the thought with a healthy one. Our discussion led her to forgive herself for wanting things to be different, to acknowledge that her father and sister had done a good job, and to see the truth that she is serving her community through her devotion—a life well lived.

Marie's mantra, and new belief, was, "My mother did the best she could with time, money, resources, competing priorities, health, and mental limitations. I am better than okay, and my childhood did not keep me from being a loving successful adult. I love who I am today. All is well."

Too often I meet with clients whose made-up versions of what life should be distract them from embracing the life that they are living. What can you release, and what can you embrace?

Self-Inflicted Wound to the Heart Chakra

Nicole, a beautiful, buttoned-up woman in her sixties, came for a healing energy session. She sat upright in her chair with her back straight and her legs crossed at the ankles. Her face was calm and reserved with no expression. She looked as though she could be photographed for a magazine. Without much of an introduction, she sat forward in her chair as she faced me and abruptly declared, "I want to release everything that is old news, and everything is old news." Then she sat back as though that was all she needed to say. She looked at me like I should get on with it.

This was her first session, and yet she took the reins and directed me to begin. I asked her, "Is there anything else you would like to share?"

Nicole softly added, straight and to the point, "I have always been active. I have a full life with children and grandchildren. My husband died, and I am alone. I am getting tired. I lack the vitality to do the things I love to do. I feel stuck."

In order to get the energy flowing for the healing energy session, I shared my intuitive assessment. I said, "Dear Nicole, your heart appears to be in pain as though you are experiencing deep grief." A vision revealed a large, metal claw-like object planted deep in the back of her heart chakra, causing a severe disruption in her field.

Her calm demeanor dissolved as Nicole gazed at the floor. Her eyes teared up as she slouched in her chair, and she said, "There is one thing. I never say it out loud; it is too painful. My daughter asked me if she should marry a man who had a genetic disease. My daughter really loved him. I was honest. I told her that I would still marry her father even if I knew that he was going to die young. She married him, and now my beautiful grandchildren are at risk for that disease."

Nicole continued as though the spigot of a faucet had just been turned on. "My daughter would have listened to me if I had told her not to do it. She was confused and asked my advice. I could have kept my grandchildren safe. What was I thinking? I cannot forgive myself for this. My grandchildren have a 50 percent chance of getting this dreadful disease. My daughter is now divorced from this man, and he is not doing well. This disease is a monster. I love my grandchildren so much. They are the love and joy of my life. I cannot bear to think of them sick. I should have told her the pain would be too great and not to marry him."

Her eyes pleaded with me to find a way to release her from the grip of her heartache.

A vision and messages were revealed during the healing energy session. Angels or beings of light surrounded her and her grandchildren. They were in a bubble of white light. I saw the older boy as a healer. "He may become a physician," I said. She told me that, interestingly enough, his father and grandfather were both physicians. I saw both children as healthy adults with fulfilling lives. I could not tell her if either would contract the disease; it may not be hers to know. She loves them unconditionally, no matter what.

I informed her that the children's father was nearing his transition from this plane and that she should prepare the children gently, reading books to them like *Remember the Secret* by Elisabeth Kubler-Ross.[32] She said, "Recently, I just got an idea to read them stories about angels so that they would know that they are not alone."

I let her know that her deceased husband was orchestrating events from the afterlife and watching after her, her daughter, and her grandchildren. He said, "Our daughter needs to lighten up. She is stressed more than she needs to be. She should laugh more and enjoy life."

Nicole laughed and said, "Funny—my daughter tells me to be more like her and less like me. I told her it is the other way around. Maybe I am right."

The message from her deceased husband to her daughter was to enjoy life more, take on fewer responsibilities, and prioritize what she did. There is no need to do it all. Most of all, she needed to enjoy time with her children.

Some messages for Nicole were also transmitted:

- You would not have your grandchildren if not for the man your daughter married. The combination of genes is unique to his union with your daughter. Wishing away the advice you gave your daughter would be wishing them away too. You would have different grandchildren.

---

[32] Kubler-Ross, *Remember the Secret.* Elisabeth Kubler-Ross, MD, was a Swiss-born psychiatrist, a pioneer in near-death studies, and the author of the groundbreaking book *On Death and Dying* (1969). In this book, because a young girl named Suzy has already discovered the wonders of God, she understands the true meaning of her friend's death. This book reminds me of my early experiences with souls in the afterlife.

- The stress on your heart is compromising your health and diminishing your life force. It is time to remove this anchor from the heart and to accept your life and your life choices.
- You can use the power of your thoughts and the power of prayer to send more light and love to your grandchildren for their health and well-being.
- Ask and thank unemployed angels to protect them.

Nicole consciously decided to let go of the pain she had inflicted on herself for all these years. Her heart opened to love her family more deeply while creating more health and well-being in her energy field. She was blessed to have her grandchildren in the same town so she can spend time with them.

We discussed how sending light and love to her grandchildren is very powerful and that, by clearing her heart, more love would flow through her. She was so delighted and said she had not felt so happy in a long time. She felt light and excited about the future and that she had the power of love. Nicole was confident that she would make a difference.

The moral of the story is that these women felt empowered and hopeful for their lives after their healing energy sessions. In each of these stories, the energy balancing created an opportunity to experience wholeness. Emotions and beliefs simmering below the surface of our conscious awareness create transactions in the subtle energy bodies that can lead to dis-ease. Sometimes, this simple shift in awareness is enough to shift beliefs, to heal, and to change lives.

***

The deep relaxation that occurs in a healing energy session allows discordant energy to be released. The most common comment I hear from clients is, "I feel like myself." Once in this state of vibrational autonomy, an opening can form to hear inner guidance. What do you choose in your life? How do you spend your time? With whom do you spend your time and why? Do you express who you really are? Do you add value to those you love? Is a limiting belief preventing you from living your life to its fullest?

You can embrace, release, and receive grace. Simply state your intention with your full conscious awareness from the center of your heart.

"I choose to embrace beliefs that are for my highest possibilities and best good."

"I choose to release limiting beliefs that no longer serve me."

"I choose to receive the grace and love available to me."

Your subconscious hears your request and takes you seriously. You can choose to release fear, self-doubt, and lack of worthiness and to open your heart and soul to receive grace from the infinite loving Source. Why not choose to love the world and yourself more? I have observed five essential steps to heal, which I call the Five Stages of Healthy Living:

1. **Self-reflection:** Enter into a still, deep, and sacred place inside of yourself. Breathe slowly and calmly to reflect on who you are, what you are, what you need, and the gifts you share with the world. You can do this in many ways. You can sit quietly, take a walk, meditate, or journal. Observe the first thing that comes to mind. The mind cannot hold you in an unhealthy pattern against your will. You get to choose your thoughts; if you do not like a thought, observe it, acknowledge it, and then choose a healthier thought.

   Declare that it is time to be free in your thoughts!

2. **Clear Out:** What beliefs about you or your life came to mind during your self-reflection? Maybe you had a tough childhood or a bad marriage or no one ever loved you enough. You are not who you are because of your story. You are who you are because of your perception of your story. It is your perception that creates a limiting belief, such as "I will never find someone who loves me." If you are no longer a child or in a bad marriage, you can give up a limiting belief that holds you in a lower vibration or low self-esteem. Whatever your belief is, you can change it.

   Free your mind and emotions from limiting beliefs and thoughts!

3. **Play:** It is time to write your new story and establish your beliefs about what is true about you today. Why not go out and play your

note and notice who hears and responds, like a jam session? Be curious about the beauty of who you are; explore your relationships, lifestyle, career, and commitments. As a mother you could take a walk in nature with your children to collect leaves and rocks and create a fairy garden at your house. A working woman with children can sing a silly song on the commute and guess what color vegetables they will have for dinner. You can drive to the beach, park, or forest and run and skip. You can turn on some music and dance and sing or make up the words to your own song. Do the work to align your essence with activities that light you up. You can identify where you lose your power and love yourself to make conscious choices to play more.

Have fun and laugh as often as you can to balance this hard work.

4. **Create:** Once you know who you are, what you are, what you need, and the gifts you have to share with the world, create your symphony. Find people, places, and things that resonate with you. As you build your authority, say yes when you mean yes and no when you mean no. Say yes when your heart sings and no when your heart tightens.

For example, if every month you meet with a group of people who like to drink, gossip, and get really loud but your interests change at some point and you discover that would prefer to go to yoga, to the gym, or to take a Spanish class, then just do it. It is okay to say, "No, thank you. Not today." You can take an art or cooking or language class and meet new people who resonate with you.

Create healthy boundaries and experience unlimited freedom.

5. **Be in the World and Live:** The last stage of healthy living is to emanate your essence in collaboration with the universe to live the meaningful life you are meant to live. For me, to really live means that I can be me in every situation. I know who I am, so I am confident, gracious, and kind to others because I love me and I am kind, gracious, and loving to myself. I get a lot of practice every day. As you shine your light in the world, you build capacity

to love the world more. Believe you are exactly where you need to be; you have become you in all your essence.

You can handle crisis and drama from a balanced, loving state of harmony among yourself, nature, and the universe. From this state of harmony, you will see people, places, and things more clearly and set your priorities on what is truly important. This is a beautiful state, and as you share your gifts from a place of peace and calm, then negative people cannot knock you off balance. You accept where they are more easily; you know it is not personal.

Welcome home!

Luckily for us, life gives us opportunities every day to stretch our ability to handle change, to avoid holding stress in our bodies, and to monitor our beliefs, thoughts, words, and actions. Remember to make conscious choices and when possible choose a word or thought of a higher vibration such as gratitude, love, compassion, awe of nature, art, or music. Every choice sets a vibration in motion with its infinite number of reactions. Choices to smile or frown, to be gracious or rude, and to be kind or inpatient are choices that affect us all.

The other day I observed a verbal altercation between two very close friends that really hit home. I felt the pain in the person who was yelling. I also felt the discomfort and disbelief in the other. It was clearly uncomfortable for everyone. I did not take sides or try to discern who was right. I was able to calm them both by acknowledging their positions and pointing out how important each is to the other. At one time in my life, I would have focused on the content of the argument and lost the importance of their relationship.

Athletes, musicians, singers, writers, and artists practice for hours every day to hone their skills. Individuals who become masters at their devotion have passion and clarity about their goals. They do not sit around saying "I want to be a published author." They say, "I am going to be a published author." They have confidence. They just know it is possible; they have faith in themselves. So they can respond automatically. They bypass their thinking brains to allow inner wisdom and their natural ability to meld as they perform. So too does creating the life you truly want take focused, conscious intention, perseverance, commitment, faith, and daily practice.

The skills of an expert are exhibited with ease, and you can be an expert too. Every day you can reflect, clear out, create, play, and be in the world as *you* to establish rhythm in your life. A state of peace and calm can become your default setting if you work at it one step at a time. The dance of life can be fun. Let your spirit dance with the universe!

CHAPTER 17
Stand in Your Power

After decades of focused spiritual development, meditation, and healing myself and others, I found myself in an abyss of misery. I felt like I was looking up into the heavens for answers that I should have already known. My husband, David, and I lived separate lives, causing strain on my finances, lifestyle, and living situation. I did not feel like I had a home. He lived the life of a bachelor, doing what he wanted, when he wanted, with whom he wanted. I pieced my life together between a rent house near work to lessen my one-hour commute and living with my son and his teenage daughters on my days off.

David helped my father out every week and was present for our children and grandchildren. We had reasons to see each other every week and had good times and many tense conversations, yet the foundation of our family was strong. The truth is that we were clearly not on the same page after nearly forty years. I was going through the motions of my day since our separation. I stayed busy to avoid loneliness.

Through the lens of a married woman in a stable, long-term relationship, my life drastically changed. Powerless, I was knocked off my feet. At the same time, an intestinal flu ravaged my body. Powerlessness can affect digestive functions and the solar plexus chakra. I had lost my power. Or then again, it could have just been the flu.

My physical body was not able to eat or be nourished. Exhausted, I called out sick from work and went to bed. I had nothing to do but lament as I lay in bed. A needle on the record player in my head was stuck on the same verse: *Why me? How did I get here? What is next?* Emotions swept through my body as I dwelled on living alone and starting my life over. I had no clear plan for my Kathi-ness. The song "No Roots" kept running through my head. My overthinking and overdoing in my distress had forced an incubation of my spirit. I was not able to hear my inner voice. I wondered if this obligatory stillness was a message to quiet my mind and listen to my heart.

As tears ran down my face, a wrenching knot in the pit in my stomach caused a sharp ache. An involuntary, violent force drew my abdomen toward my spine. To lessen the pain, I stilled my breath. My chest was frozen, and I did not breathe. There was no air going in or out, no time, and no space. I could not move the needle to the next groove or play a new song.

Suddenly after several minutes, my body was forced to exhale as though against my will. I choked on my own breath. I swallowed the sobs in my throat. "I am fine," I offered as condolence to myself as my tears streamed down my face and soaked my pillow.

My tears cleansed my soul and spirit as a cathartic expression of my grief. I did not realize I held such grief, anger, and pain. A weight was lifted off my chest. After minutes, hours, or more—I do not know—I smiled a genuine, mouth-turned-up smile. My breath moved easily between my lips. I was grateful to be me. What had just happened? I felt light, whole, renewed, and ready to move forward. I thought, *Kathi is getting her groove back. I choose to love the world. I am of the world. I love me!*

Beings of light swept me away to a dream world where I sensed the palpable presence of their love. I sensed my heart open a little more than a crack as universal light and love flowed in. My friends tell me that a when a heart shatters, it opens to love the world more. I was opening to love the world more.

I visualized the violet ray as it spread throughout my etheric body and biofield. The violet ray is used for protection from a negative or low frequency emitted from people, places, things, and environments, and it transmutes that negativity into the universal light. Its frequency is that of the seventh chakra, connecting to divine wisdom and purpose. This high frequency clears the physical, emotional, and mental subtle energy bodies.

My entire body vibrated at the frequency of the violet ray. With a calm breath and a quiet mind, I repeated an affirmation slowly: "All is well." As the discordant energy around me dissolved, I was reborn. My throat chakra softened and cleared. I found my voice in a loving, kind way, devoid of anger. In this magical moment, I felt free to be me.

I sensed the old stuck energy in my body dissolve into a fine mist. I floated into an etheric mist beyond my body. In the mist I heard my guides say, "Your divine light deserves your unconditional love and attention."

The real questions before me were clear. Who do I really want to be? What do I need? How do I want to share my gifts with the world? I thought that not needing to check in with anyone else to make plans, eat dinner, or spend money had its advantages. My perception of my husband's choices softened. His choices were not wrong; I was not right. I would no longer challenge or interfere with his lifestyle and relationships.

I chose to freely accept that his relationship with another woman was not going to work for me. He could not convince me otherwise. I set a clear boundary: "Leave her, or we cannot be together." He said that no one could tell him what to do. We had both drawn our lines in the sand, so there was nothing left to argue about.

We both expressed that we did not want either of us to compromise who we were. We respect our family ties and history together. I did not want him to change for me. I am free to be me. Sixty is the new forty, right? I am ready to live my life as I am. I am ready!

Victorious as an author, healer, speaker, mother, and friend, I am becoming me! The fear dissolved, and the crazy, angry woman inside me seemed to vanish too. I was excited to express my Kathi-ness. I found meaningful activities with friends, selflessly expressing love for myself.

I was spontaneous. I would go out to dinner, plays, and concerts; cook dinner for my friends; attend lectures at The Mount; go on an owl prowl, snowshoeing on a moonlit night; and teach classes on developing intuition. I even went to Marblehead for the weekend by myself, where I met some lovely women. We shared lunch at the beach, walks, dinner, and talks. I exchanged healing energy sessions with a crystal singing bowl healer. I woke up in the middle of the night, turned on the light, got out my laptop, and worked on my book.

I felt like I was reliving the seventies, when I was in college. Friends would invite me to stay at their houses, and we would just hang out. We could talk for hours about metaphysical topics, spirituality, and our life-affirming experiences that had shaped us. As I unwrapped buried treasures within me, I found stamina, trust, and acceptance of what I need in a relationship and my life. Nothing was lost; a new future was being formed.

A sense of something wonderful had filled my spirit. I felt illuminated. My friends, colleagues, family, and husband commented, "You seem different—happy and confident." They could see my glow.

No more victim! The change in my perception was liberating. I have a wonderful place to live, kind neighbors, a supportive family, precious friends, and a growing vocation that I love. It is time to manifest the reality I want. Perhaps I will find a cottage or condo in the Berkshires when the time is right, but the house on Fairfield Street is holding me gently and singing to me now. The wind chimes play a sweet tune of joy with each magical breeze. All is well!

***

I told you my story to highlight the importance of moving forward even when your life is at its darkest. When you find joy and companionship and ignite your inner light, you can be victorious too.

Where do you lose your power? The divine light within you is a jewel, always beautiful and powerful. Remnants of your thoughts, emotions, words, and perceptions are held in your energy body and field. You will never forget misfortunes, deaths, betrayals, or losses. The lessons we learn about ourselves and our choices provide us with wisdom to guide us toward our future.

You do really matter to yourself and to the people with whom you share your world; it is a truth. You can set lamentation aside. It goes nowhere. Instead, deploy light and love to the part of you where you sense fear, hate, or anger. The light within you will expand, pushing away the emotions that no longer serve you, just as it did for me. You have the power too.

Once you know how to send light and love to yourself, you can then send light to others in your life, to a situation where you do not feel heard, or to someone to whom you are afraid to speak your truth. Everything is energy, so sending the energy of light and love can affect the energy of a situation, person, place, or thing. Try it and notice whether anything changes. The blessing comes when you shine your essence into the world. You attract that essence back toward you. Remember, like attracts like.

In order to heal loved ones, you need to fill them with this loving light.

Remember only their strengths and the times they were successful, kind, loving and playful until all acts of goodness are exhausted. You keep the healing energy in a high vibration by only recounting their strengths. You never mention an indiscretion or criticize or ridicule during a healing. This is how you honor and revive a loved one.

Most of all, you need to have faith that the divine light within your loved one exists and that you can reach it with your love. Healing requires cooperation. When you demand, plead, or bargain with the universe, it does not work so well. Make a promise to yourself that you will not break to align with the universe.

Can you bring to your conscious mind one thing that you will never break the promise with yourself? You can fill in the blank with your own thoughts. These are mine.

I will never say I am afraid to be alone to myself. I choose to love myself.

I will never think it is my fault that someone doesn't love me. I choose to speak helpful thoughts to myself.

I will never allow myself to think less of myself even when others do.

You are a unique essence. You are not the guilt, shame, or blame you may have experienced. Leave one thing on this page right now. Stop and think: it can be something small, a baby step.

"I will never say my thighs are fat. I love my thighs exactly as they are."

You can choose to be proud to be *you*! Others will see you as you see yourself. Your ability to heal happens from the inside out, not the outside in. One day the physical body will no longer exist. It is important to love yourself. Love is power; hurt and anger are power too. The true meaning of giving grace to yourself is to honor your sacred journey. Every belief, thought, and act has the power to either give life force or take life force away. Your power should be used wisely.

Choose to love the world and love yourself. Shine your jewel-like essence in the world. Embrace the power of love.

Chapter 18
The Power Within to Heal

A sense of helplessness can be overwhelming. We can only really manage our own lives, yet we want the best for our loved ones. There are times when we have no options but to sit idly by to watch and wait for them to thrive, survive, or in some cases die. It takes great courage and love to hold a healing space while our loved ones struggle. The following is a story of a parent who loved her child unconditionally and would do anything to heal him.

Please Let Me Be

Jane came to me for a healing energy session to help her relax and sleep better at night. She had tired, dull eyes yet sat with her back straight as her mouth formed a warm, gracious smile. She told me, "I have been happily married for a long time. My husband and I are looking forward to travel in our retirement years. I just retired this year. I have planned well for retirement. I now have time and money to do the things I was not able to do while working." She continued with her story: "I live in a lovely, well-appointed home with gardens and a sun room for plants. It is my sanctuary." She stated, "I am here for healing energy because I am not sleeping well. I worked so hard all my life. I want to enjoy my retirement. I am just so tired from not sleeping."

She had a reserved, graceful demeanor, wearing a long cashmere sweater over a turtleneck and slim-fitting pants. She was clearly articulate and exuded confidence. I asked her what else was going on in her life because everything sounded so wonderful. Her shoulders softened, and her dull eyes moistened as she said, "There is one piece of my life that is unsettled. What to do about my son?"

She described her son, saying, "He is nearly thirty years old and has been addicted to substances for over a decade. He has been in and out of rehabilitation programs, bounced among colleges, had several unfulfilling work experiences and messy relationships." She said, "I cannot sleep due to worry. Every day I wake up wondering what is the next situation where I will need to bail him out."

Jane's body visibly tensed, and her eyes filled with tears as she methodically described her relationship with her son over the past decade. She said, "I offer positive feedback when he is on track and solutions when he stumbles. I set the appropriate boundaries when he is actively using. I ask him to leave the house. I don't think he is always honest with me. How can I trust him?"

As I am able to communicate with deceased souls by interpreting the energy field of the deceased person, I also can communicate with the souls of the living by tuning into their energy fields. The following are the messages for Jane that came from the spirit of her son:

> You just want to help me so that you can put me in a box and stop having to do things for me. It is all about you. I can feel your fear and worry. You do not think that I can make it without you. I need to do this myself. Empower me; believe in me; see me five years from now successful, sober, happy, and free of this demon. See me—please see me. I got this for better or worse; this is my journey. If you make every decision for me, where will I be? How can I be on my own? I will make mistakes. Let me! Be there for me. I love you.

He continued with passion behind his words.

> You see me as a weak addict, taking your time, money, and resources, upsetting your well-organized life. Well, this is me. Let me be. I will ask for help when I need it. Do not judge me! You cannot tie me up in a bow so

166

you can say, "All done. Now on with my life." You are so selfish. You cannot bear the pain of having a son who is an addict and not your version of success. If you do not believe I can make it, maybe I cannot. What if you are right? Why bother if I cannot make it? I want to make my own decisions. I hate that I am stuck in my mother's web. I want to be financially independent, a respected member of the community. Why do you think I beat myself up and numb my mind by taking more drugs? Sometimes I think to myself, *If I do not try to succeed, then I cannot fail.* I am just not ready to risk failure.

I could sense his fragile and tender heart. I relayed the conversation to Jane, who was in disbelief. She had no idea how her fear and worry was affecting him. She confirmed, "I love him unconditionally and only want what is best for him—to be sober and happy."

I asked her to close her eyes and envision him in two, three, and five years, if she could stretch that far into the future. She said, "I cannot see past his present existence with a troubled girlfriend, living here and there, using now and then, unemployed and lost."

I told her, "If you expect him to fail, he may keep failing." I explained that fear is a frequency that attracts more of the same frequency. Her thoughts were planting seeds of doubt, which were fed by her worry and fears. She was actually making it harder for him to raise his frequency to the level of his needs for success. "Try to see his possibilities," I implored.

She resisted, "I am afraid to attach to an illusion that is not true and then be disappointed." The situation was anathema to her.

I offered her my thoughts. "When he hears how disappointed you are in him, he loses sight of loving himself and does not feel lovable. His inner work is to dive into his heart chakra. But it is painful there, so he continues to avoid sobriety. When the mind craves, shames, and blames, the cycle persists."

I continued to describe the effects occurring beneath the surface of her rational mind in the nonphysical world. Drug use fosters a state of illusion, a separation from the voice of the heart and intuition that cannot be heard through the fog. A union of the heart and mind with true desire can rewire the circuits in the brain.

Our physical reality is not enough to combat this confusion on how to solve the inner conflict. What to do when the mind and heart are not in sync? We must love them and invoke help from the invisible world.

Wishing things were different for her son along with fearing and worrying developed a sense of helplessness that led to poor sleep and low energy. Jane had power within herself to heal her son in the invisible world of love. She could be proactive and affect the energy field around her son through a daily reflection with the belief that he is happy, financially stable, and capable of a healthy, long-term relationship. The projection of her positive thoughts into the future could create a pathway toward a healthy life for her son.

Jane realized that she could keep pushing him uphill and remain exhausted and disillusioned, or she could fill him with love so that he might float above his current situation. Jane agreed to accept his past behaviors as part of his journey. She understood that he is not the behaviors. He is a unique essence of light having an earthly experience. Friends and family would see him the way she saw him and he saw himself.

There are many paths to many truths that provide a shift in our consciousness that may not otherwise be available to us. We all have free will to choose our paths, for better or worse. Jane's son may decide not to move forward and to exit this world; that would be his choice. If he does, then he will need more light for that transition. Perhaps there is a treasure to be opened at a later date, a blessing that she cannot see today. Who knows what choices her son will make when he is aligned with his true essence?

Her son could be her teacher. Jane came to understand that how she interprets and responds to people, situations, and life events *tells* us about who she is and her soul journey. She is meant to learn from her life, to move on, and to live a full life. Although this is easier said than done, when she accepts what is, it leaves nothing to forgive. To be thankful for her lessons, even the ones that brought her to her knees, takes courage, perseverance, commitment, and love for herself. When she embraces these truths for herself, she can share her wisdom with her son to empower him.

I told her, "You can honor yourself too and know you have done more than enough. Sleep well at night, dear one. No matter the reason for healing, it is always the same; pure, unconditional love heals all wounds and makes us whole." This is true even if the outcome is different than we want. We cannot see the whole picture of the universe from where we stand.

I suggested that she ask him to tell her his dreams and desires with as much detail as possible. If he can sense it, taste it, feel it, hear it, and imagine it, then it is possible. She should ask him how he would feel if it was true in this moment. The more he states his dreams, the more reprogramming occurs. Let him tell his story, with more detail to better to create his vision. Healing starts in the invisible world of imagination, magic, and hope. I do not know if she did this or not, but at least I planted the seed.

His success already exists in the greater universe where all things are possible; he just needs to recalibrate his life to align with that possibility. Jane can light up his future and surround him in love and light for his journey. It is the greatest gift that she can give him.

She had tried everything she knew to try, so maybe believing in him will shift his pattern of poor choices. Purposely shaping and building thought forms through conscious intention may lead him out and eventually keep him safe. It takes a leap of faith to trust in his free will, mind, heart, imagination, and courage. Together we asked angels to guide and protect her son on his journey.

The following messages came through for Jane:

- Do not create expectations or outcomes.
- Resist the urge to swoop in and save the day.
- Create a safety net during tough times without needing to steer the ship.
- Allow the universal consciousness to absorb your fear, worry, and doubt.
- Be a witness and allow him to feel the self-love that comes with self-empowerment.
- Fill your heart with love for self and your child.
- Sleep well at night knowing that you did all you could do and accept that he is a soul on his own journey.
- Surrender the power to the universe, where healing already exists.

This is the affirmation that I suggested to Jane: "Empower me to be free to move on, and empower my son to choose his life wisely."

***

You are already creating your reality with your beliefs and thoughts. Use deliberate intention to change your world. Your choices led you to where you are and can lead you out. You have the power within to change your reality. Choose your thoughts wisely. Try it! Then note what shifts in your world.

Through a peaceful nature, hope, courage, and intuition, you can move past seemingly unsurmountable challenges. Our journey on earth in this incarnation has been speckled with sorrow, pain, disappointment, love, and joyous times. What fills you with joy empowers your life force.

Each person is whole, perfect, and complete; the only effort is in the remembering. To remember, I dissolve feelings of helplessness through deep meditation, prayer, and a focused intention, melting into the essence of me, my Kathi-ness. Just saying these words raises my vibrational autonomy in alignment with my true essence.

Try it. Say. "I am whole, perfect, and complete in my __(your name)_ -ness." Now you really have to believe it. Repeat this truth over and over to change the electromagnetic waves in your energy body and empower yourself to be you. Feel the difference so quickly and completely as you activate your power within!

These are some affirmations for overcoming helplessness:

- "I have courage within me to face my fears."
- "I am inspired to experience new ways of being."
- "I laugh at myself freely."
- "I trust my intuition and follow my inner guidance."

CHAPTER 19
Mother Nature and Miracles

The single most important thing you can do to connect to your spirit; to release what no longer serves you; to witness miracles; and to invite in the light, love, and energy of the heavens and earth is to be in nature. Most people do not commune with nature often enough. Being disconnected from nature is unhealthy. Here's why and how to fix it.

Would you like to see a miracle in your life? Simply pause to view the night sky, the sunrise, the flowers blooming, the children playing, the fresh berries in the summer, or the snow-covered evergreens in the winter. The patterns, colors, and textures observed in our natural world are miracles. A million cells divide and regenerate continuously. The sunlight, water, nutrient-rich soil, and weather conditions have to be just right to create the miracles we observe in nature. Nature heals.

Mother Earth and all of nature vibrate at the frequency of love, healing, peace, and calm. When the mind focuses on the scents, textures, colors, birds, and animals in the woods, oceans, deserts, or mountains, the mind becomes clear. The unobstructed energy flow of the trees, the plants, the fields, the skies, and the stars can calm emotions by focusing our attention on nature. The physical body also responds with a sense of peace that can provide clarity to relax the mind.

Our ability to ground to the earth is essential for health and well-being. Think about your laptop that can only work as long as the battery is charged. Once you lose the charge, you have to plug it in. The human body can only hold so much charge. The earth is a large electromagnetic object with an infinite power source. Physicians perform electrocardiograms

(EKG)[33] and electroencephalograms (EEG)[34] to detect electrical activity in our hearts and brains.

As electrical human beings, we are innately wired to discharge excess charges into the earth, like an electrical outlet that needs to be grounded. The earth absorbs excess charges associated with stress effortlessly. It is the magic of nature. As human beings living on earth, it is important that we to learn to ground. It is a win-win to receive the life force from the earth as she absorbs excess charges in our bodies. Through conscious intention, we can discharge the charge of anxiety through our feet into the earth.

In the book *Barefoot Wisdom: Better Health through Grounding* by Anne Marie Chiasson, MD, [35] you will learn many ways to commune with nature and the rich resources available in Mother Earth. According to Dr. Chiasson, grounding is a freely available way to tap into the Earth's always-accessible and ever-powerful natural energy to rebalance the body and restore health.

Many individuals are prone to be in their heads and not in their physical bodies. We often hear people telling us to ground ourselves, but we may not be sure what that means and how we might do it. One of the easiest ways to begin is to bring your attention to your breath as it enters and leaves your body. A full conscious awareness of your body with the intention to be grounded is facilitated as you breathe slowly. This focused intention creates a flow of energy throughout the body. After several breaths, you will probably find that you feel more connected to your

---

[33] Mayo Clinic, "Electrocardiogram (ECG or EKG)," accessed April 22, 2019, retrieved from https://www.mayoclinic.org/tests-procedures/ekg/about/pac-20384983. An electrocardiogram records the electrical signals in your heart. It's a common test used to detect heart problems and monitor the heart's status in many situations.

[34] Mayo Clinic, "EEG (electroencephalogram)," accessed April 22, 2019 retrieved from https://www.mayoclinic.org/tests-procedures/eeg/about/pac-20393875. An electroencephalogram (EEG) is a test that detects electrical activity in your brain using small, metal discs (electrodes) attached to your scalp. Your brain cells communicate via electrical impulses and are active all the time, even when you're asleep. This activity shows up as wavy lines on an EEG recording.

[35] Sharon Whiteley and Ann Marie Chiasson, MD, *Barefoot Wisdom: Better Health through Grounding, 1ˢᵗ Edition* (Atglen, Pennsylvania: Red Feather Mind, Body Spirit, 2018).

physical body. As you begin to feel comfortable in your body, connect your full conscious awareness to nature. You can get things done, think clearly, and calm your emotions when you are grounded—things that would not be possible when your energy is swirling around.

For me, a walk in the woods or on a beach creates a sense of peace. I often bring home a rock or a seashell with its energetic imprint to recreate a sense of peace. Wherever you are, you can imagine a sacred place in nature and transform your energy body. You can imagine in your mind's eye, as you breathe in slowly with your full conscious awareness, a place you have been or always wanted to go, whether it is make-believe or real. Let the place become real to you as you observe the lush or austere surroundings, the precious scents, the rich colors, the various textures, the musical sounds, the feeling of air on your skin, or the warmth of the sun.

A wealth of healing energy is available to you through the healing effects of nature at all times, twenty-four hours a day, seven days a week. Your focused mind can recreate the experience, and your body responds as though you are in nature. As you observe the sensations within your body, you are experiencing the miracle of life on our planet.

Once you experience a sense of peace, with your full conscious intention send the sensation through your entire body, permeating every cell, and then fill the spaces between the cells. Use your mind's eye and your imagination to bathe your energy body with the wholeness of nature. Your mind's intention transforms energy into physical matter and creates a sense of peace in the body. You are a powerful being of light. As you experience this sense of wholeness, you know that it is true. This is not a mental exercise; it is experiential. I invite you to embrace the truth that healing is always near, within our minds and our environment. It is your birthright!

Miracles are closer than you think! You can physically connect to nature by walking barefoot and feeling the sensation of the earth through the bottom of your feet. The most benefit you can get from your experience is to be fully present. The earth is a large electromagnetic object, and you can connect easily from the top floor of a multistory building, in a plane, or on a boat in the ocean. When you ground to Mother Earth, you relieve dis-ease in the body, mind, and emotions.

Another way to bring the balanced energy of nature into your body is to imagine you are a plant or tree. A plant does not worry that the sun will not shine; it spreads its roots deep into the earth regardless. It reaches toward the sun without distraction. It is not angry with the weather, the soil, or other plants that grow nearby. The plant does not want a gardenia to be a rose. It accepts all plants as they are. All are beautiful. You can plant some flowers and watch them grow or walk in the forest and notice the foliage or sit by a river and watch it flow. You will reap many silent rewards.

Your imagination can create flow in your subtle energy bodies. Can you imagine that you are a river and that you can sense its freedom as it flows toward the sea? Rocks, trees, twists, and turns do not deter the water as it flows. Perhaps imagine you are floating on a river if that is easier. Maybe you are on the rainbow river for healing. Why not? It is your imagination. You can imagine that you are on a river with every color of the rainbow swirling around you as you float. This is not meant to be a demanding process or an opportunity to berate yourself for not being good at imagining. This is an opportunity to be kind to yourself as you explore new ways to experience yourself as an energy being in the world of nature and magic. It can be fun!

Daffodils sprout from a dormant bulb, and caterpillars dissolve and crystalize into a new form out of your sight. Resisting the natural flow of life because your rational mind cannot see the details is a fool's journey. Instead you enjoy the beauty of the daffodil's flower and the butterfly's flight. Subatomic particles of light are moving, and your world is ever-changing, even if you cannot see it. My point is for you to go with the flow of life and see what happens.

Where do you want to bloom or fly? It cannot hurt to try in this moment, just for this one little moment, to imagine and set your intention for what you want to manifest. Then consider that the possibility already exists for whatever you choose to imagine—a healthy body, a better job, and a loving relationship. The subtle particles of the universe will flow beneath the surface of your physical reality to meet you there. You can create miracles through your imagination. What if it was true today? What would it feel like?

The subtle energy bodies are receiving the benefit of your imagination even if your rational mind cannot register the change instantly. I am saying all this about nature because so many people I see cannot get out of their heads. Their limiting self-talk sounds like, "This is me and has always been me and will always be me. I cannot change, and you cannot teach an old dog new tricks." The first step for an old dog may be to dissolve the limiting belief that it is an old dog and can experience a miracle. Why not you? You are always free in your mind to choose your thoughts and your beliefs.

Your thoughts can be examined. Are they true today? There is great power in self-awareness and understanding that which you hold to be true, that which you want to be true, and that which is true. You can choose to bring flow to your life by simplifying the demands on your time, accepting what is, and focusing on what is truly important.

The following is one of the most common struggles for younger people today. The realization that we are electrical beings and grounding to the earth is helpful.

Not Grounded, Too Much Anxiety

Mary Ann was referred to me by a client for a distance healing session. I spoke to her on the phone to describe the distance session, to hear her story, and to set our expectations for the session. Her voice was loud and intense, and her words were deliberate and forceful. "I want a relationship in my life. I am afraid I will never find anyone and will be alone forever. My anxiety is overwhelming. I cannot think straight. I deserve a promotion at work, and I keep getting passed over. Why is this happening to me? What am I supposed to be doing in my life? I am stuck." These are common complaints for individuals seeking a healing energy session.

I could sense the intensity of her anxiety in her physical body, although we were well over a thousand miles apart. I asked her about a spiritual practice. She said, "I am spiritual and have many spiritual friends who are clairvoyant and psychic. We meet regularly to evolve our intuition and our ability to connect to spirit. I want to eat better and lose weight, too." She described in great detail how she was not recognized at work for her contributions and how unfair it was. She did not like to exercise and rarely got outside to walk, and she wanted to improve her food choices.

As she revealed her story, I sensed a dense mass of energy moving from her lower spine up through the top of her head. This rigidity in her spine was as intense as her communication style. I sensed that her biofield was filled with the same dense charge associated with anxiety. The charges I sensed in her head were also intense.

My intuitive assessment revealed that she was not grounded to the earth and had a limited energy flow through her ankles, knees, and hips. The joints in the legs can become congested due to a fear of moving forward and not being able to stand on one's own two feet. Her sacral and solar plexus chakras had an excessive spin. Also, her heart chakra was pulled to the right, indicating too much responsibility, authority, and physical world demands versus the feminine, softer side of life. She is disconnected from her heart and soul.

I used guided imagery to assist her core energy to descend deep into the earth. The earth absorbed the excess charge and neutralized the charges in her body, mind, and heart. In this moment, she filled her heart with the love available to her from the earth and felt safe in her body. The ego released the need to know, to be right, and to control situations, people, or things. She surrendered to her true self.

Some messages were provided for Mary Ann:

- The intellect can be so confident that the mind is right that the heart cannot be heard. The intuition from her heart and her feminine energy were trivialized and disregarded as not important or weak at the subconscious level. In the past, she had relied on her intellect to direct and gauge her activities. She overcompensated so that she could prove to the world that she did not have the individual self-determination of a jellyfish—clearly lacking trust in her heart and self-worth. The feminine and masculine energies were out of balance.
- A battle between the mind and the heart is a tough one. The heart's only defense is love, and its offense is love. The mind uses intellect and rationalization and is so busy that it does not always stop long enough to consider that the heart may have an answer. The mind is limited to what has been experienced, programmed, or remembered. It is only through the heart that you can know your soul. The ego can twist messages and cause suffering and overreactions. The heart allows and accepts what is, calming

emotions and the mind so a pathway can appear. When a solution based on the heart's essence comes to the surface of consciousness, true power is expressed.

- Get out and at least walk every day; move your body and go outside to spend some time in nature. The integration of your body and life responsibilities with your soul takes courage, patience, guidance, trust, faith, and the wanting to be whole. It is essential for your healing to commune with nature and consciously ground to the earth.

- Try a softer voice and consciously listen to others. Slowing down the speed of the conversation alone can develop an appreciation for others so that you can open your heart to them. An open heart that is listening can avoid igniting anger and impatience with others.

- It sounds like your psychic friends would be a great place to build a steady companionship of kindred spirits. They can help to kindle insight into who you really are in a safe, comfortable place. As you speak, act, and express your version of your truths, you can check it against the truths of your group. Ask for feedback and listen so that you can build close bonds in relationships.

The following will help you to integrate your mind, heart, and soul to create miracles.

- Ground deep into the core of Mother Earth every day.
- Invoke the healing power of nature available to you.
- Seek quietude to hear your soul's desire.
- Strengthen your capacity to create community. You never have to be alone.

Love is needed to balance a strong intellect, and more love is available right below your nose and feet. You know the saying: the answer is right under your nose. Look down at your feet and past your nose, and what do you see? The earth. Be true to your heart, love yourself, and love your life. And remember that you are never alone. You have help from spirit guides, angels, family, friends, and most of all Mother Nature.

***

The power within us to heal creates miracles that I am blessed to witness in my practice. I have observed that the true power to find joy and peace comes from what you believe and subsequently say to yourself. What story do you tell yourself when you feel disempowered? Mary Ann said that no one recognized her contributions at work and she lacked trust in the universe that there would be a partner for her. She blamed the external world when in fact her heart could tell her another story—to love herself.

Your story is generated from your experiences, your thoughts about those experiences, your reactions to those experiences, and your entrenched beliefs about those experiences. Your mind can create a story about you that may simply not be true. Consider what you learn about yourself when you lose your power. Do you go on and on about what you would say to the person to whom you lost your power? Do you tell all your friends your version of the story with emotion, facts, arguments, and fabrications? Anywhere you intervene in this cycle can be the first step on a path of healing. See the appendix for an exercise to handle anxiety.

***

Nature is both simple and complex at the same time and yet finds its own beautiful balance. So too are our lives both simple and complex. Our challenge is to organically find the balance, flowing with that which we cannot change and making conscious choices to change what we can, especially when it is the complexity of our own minds that pulls us out of balance, as with the woman in the previous story.

Consciously choosing to connect to nature can remind you of the simplicity of things and invite your soul to find peace in the moment. A simpler life allows your inner voice to rise above the noise of a demanding external environment by reducing the number of moving parts and distractions that are driven by the ego. These complexities can not only lack substance to enrich your life; they can drain the rich resource of your life force. Simplicity is a sacred invitation to be *you*, honoring yourself.

Complex, productive lives are different than busy, chaotic lives. You can be busy and balanced as long as you live a conscious life that includes self-care, nutritious foods from nature, exercise, and leisure time with family and friends, time outdoors, peaceful sleep, and a daily spiritual practice. A conscious life has a spiritual purpose beyond the physical world's demands of having and doing more—a purpose to share love, compassion, and appreciation and a practice to be a witness to suffering while not taking on the suffering. We are beings of light having an earthly experience, not human beings having a spiritual experience.

What would you change in your life to create more time and space to express your unique gifts with your family, friends, colleagues, neighbors, and community? To be you, expressing your *you*-ness in the world. A simple life invites activities that support balance so that you can be fully present and want to give more and share your love with others. Can you imagine what in your life you would need to change to have a simpler life? Is there a way to bring an experience of nature into your daily routine?

Not knowing the answer, by the way, is okay. You will know when you are in the moment and curious about your surroundings. You will become more alert and notice what resonates with you. What comes to mind as you look around your home? Do you wonder about the color, the texture, the artwork, the furniture, the window treatments, and how they make you feel? How would you enhance your home to reflect your sacred gifts and inner essence? Can you make a conscious choice in this moment that allows you to bring one new thing into your home to reflect who you are? You can clean out the clutter that lowers your frequency; clean out a closet, drawer, or room and create a sacred space to meditate, pray, or just be.

There is an old sycamore tree on the property where I work. I walk to meet it face to face, often leaning against it when I meditate. The circumference of the tree requires five adults with their arms stretched out wide to wrap around the trunk. I have deep respect for the old sycamore and its long life. I wonder about all the people who have spoken to this tree and received guidance. I hike Monument Mountain, which offers a spectacular view from the summit, and am in awe of the rocks and ledges, as well as the ferns that grow in such little soil. The roots of trees wrap around rocks, holding on for dear life. It is magical.

The view from my bedroom window of the farmland and mountains behind them has never disappointed me in the morning. The magic of a brilliant sunset and sunrise touches me deeply as I respect the movement of the earth as it turns each day. Mary Ann from the story above shared with me that when she walks on the beach and picks up shells, she feels the power of the universe. This is her sacred place.

Ask your sacred, divine self to take a moment in reflection to notice where reverence, respect, astonishment, devotion, dedication, commitment, or enthusiasm show up for you. Where does your sacred light want to expand? You can tell by whether or not you get a welcoming electromagnetic charge as you bring to mind the alternatives. What stirs your soul? Where are you being pulled? Maybe what you seek is not so far from your reach when you start to examine the steps to make something happen. Maybe you dream of playing tennis and wonder how that would ever happen. Then you realize, *Well, I need to find a tennis club and take lessons.*

If you are not feeling pulled in any one direction, observe your life, begin to connect the dots, and clean house, literally and figuratively inside and out. Get rid of the clutter in your mind so you can see clearly. When you decide to live life fully, there is no more time to be dimmed, depressed, silent, or waiting to act. Remember that you are always free.

You have free will, and you are a unique being of light. You can decide your own path one step at a time. You are never chained to what seems to be your current reality, lack of finances, home, or relationship. Think of one thing or thought you can change today to close the gap between status quo, failure, and success.

A less complex life requires you to release thoughts and activities that are distracting you from being you, such as worries about the future, finances, family, and children. A loop of thoughtless worry and perseveration draws on your life force, which leads to exhaustion mentally and physically. This is what happened to Mary Ann. It creates a separation from your own unique essence and the universal love available to you. So why worry and drain your life force? I ask you. Instead, spend your energy wisely.

Nature does not have a mind or emotions, yet it is complex and works out the kinks. You can too, when you go with the flow and let go of limiting thoughts and emotions. A simple meditation imagining a blue bird flying overhead can shift your energy and open your mind to free your thoughts. This is what I imagined.

> The blue bird is perfect as she flies above the hubbub of
> life undisturbed by the noise, the ruckus, and hullabaloo

of children laughing, automobiles speeding by, the noise of a television, a radio, or a computer game.

She ignores the manmade sounds and listens intently to the chorus of birds singing and the rustling branches of the trees. She witnesses the geese honking as they return in the spring. What sounds do you hear in your world? Are they pleasant like a soft wind chime purchased on vacation at a time when you felt peace and calm? You remember the vacation each time the stillness is bothered by the wind. The gentle sound does not disturb you. It is only here to remind you.

The blue bird flies above the trees, rivers, and streams and has a bird's-eye view of the land. You too can fly above the land in your mind and enter into your spirit to see your life from a new perspective.

Create your own experience of a blue bird flying overhead and remember that it is your imagination. You do not need to be literal; be free in your thoughts and imagine your life from above. If you tend to worry, imagine you are free from worry and consciously choose to disperse all your worry into the oneness, into the field of your imagination. Now you can use the precious gift of your mind to invite in that which enhances your well-being. What you focus on becomes your reality. Your mind transforms energy into physical matter. That is how we manifest our desires, not by worry.

As with families, careers, hobbies, and relationships, there is a season and a reason. You can review your life to see what has expired. Do you have regrets or limiting beliefs that are still lurking around in your subconscious that have been held past their expiration date? You would throw milk out if it expired months ago and not think twice. You would not invite old milk into your physical body and risk a stomach upset. Taking on a job, relationship, or role as a volunteer does not mean you have made a lifetime commitment. My sailboat, *Emma-Mia,* was a passion for fifteen years. One day I woke up and decided it was time to move on. I had no regrets.

My experience had enriched my life beyond measure. What in your life has expired?

Simplify your thoughts too. You can honor and respect the transitions you made through conscious choice. We all make mistakes, so honor the decisions you made in your past. Few of us would do everything exactly the same if we had life to do over. We all learn from our experiences. The alternative is beating yourself up. You may become irritable, resentful, angry, or even hateful toward an experience where you felt trapped. Simplify your thoughts that you circulate in your head. Remember instead the pleasant, fulfilling moments.

Your thoughts cannot hold you against your will. Remember that you are always free in your thoughts. There are trade-offs in life, so keep only what is worth your time and resources and what gives you joy. As with the woman in an earlier chapter, she could not experience pure joy as long as she held on to hate. Instead of recycling the past, why not focus on a sacred yearning that is being called up to the surface of your being? What wants expression now?

The conclusion is that a conflict between the heart and the mind can be terrorizing and keep you from your ability to express what you came here to do. It is always simple and yet never easy to end a cycle in an evolutionary stage of transition. However, when you let go of your past ways of doing, thinking, and being, you can open yourself to a new horizon. A miracle can just appear. The heart is the only part of you that encompasses all of you and what you are evolving into.

You can ground to the loving, nurturing energy of the earth to experience freedom from your mind. Mother Earth is the key to consciously embrace the heart so that it can be heard as it spirals toward the soul and bypasses the mind. A daily practice to consciously connect with nature either physically or in your mind's eye will bring balance and healing to your life.

The following affirmation is one I say to myself frequently: "I move forward in life with grace and ease. I am where I am supposed to be at all times. I embrace the stillness as I embrace the movement; both enlighten and expand me." This reminds me to be still and listen to my heart.

CHAPTER 20
On Joy and Living

I am a powerful being of light; you are too! *On Becoming You* presents stories of personal transformation, self-empowerment, and joyful living through an understanding of the energy and mystical laws. Consciously experiencing joy helps to connect you to your spirit and the larger picture of your life.

Joy is the experience of radiating your divine light. Where there is joy, there is no pain, sorrow, lack, or fear. A sense of no time or space prevails, and only love, light, and wholeness exist. Your inner light is always glowing, bright and beautiful, to live the joyful life you are meant to live. When in doubt, choose joy!

Imagine joy as a colossal electromagnetic object filled with universal love that draws you toward it. Without resistance, you would float into the loving arms of the universe and feel loved, safe, and nurtured. You would have to really work hard to resist its immense pull. What would that resistance be? Your thoughts and emotions of fear, victimhood, wondering *Am I enough? Am I worthy? What will I lose?* and *What will I gain?* all create resistance to receiving the frequency of joy that already exists. Remember, joy is your birthright.

I can find joy by imitating a sunflower. I turn my face toward the sun to sense the joy, warmth, and vitality as it soaks into my skin and body. Oh, the ever-present warmth of the sun fills me with joy. Even when the foundation of my Kathi-ness and marriage was dissolving, I could always find an element of joy in my surroundings. I would pause with full conscious awareness to focus on all the things that bring joy into my life until I filled my heart with my Kathi-ness. All the memories of joy in my life brought an unsolicited smile to my face as the seed of joy sprouted and blossomed in my heart. The world has so much to offer. I refuse to let fear fill my heart. I choose *joy!*

You are an energetic being receiving and sending electromagnetic particles in and around your body and field. Joy is a higher frequency than most vibrations that you experience. As you may recall from previous chapters, a higher frequency can clear out a lower frequency. Joy can clear lower frequencies from your body, leading to health and well-being.

Take a moment to reflect on the following questions. Maybe write them down so you can review them later. What are your beliefs, thoughts, activities, words, people, places, and things that unleash a sense of peace, calm, joy, and pleasure? When are you all in and nothing can distract you? What experiences do you crave—beauty, nature, art, family, learning, or travel? What spurs you to action when you are bored, lonely, or unencumbered with your routine?

It is important to know what brings you joy. Joy enhances our life force and brings clarity and focus on your life purpose.

Your memories of joy can be invited into every cell of your body. Joy is a high frequency and can clear out the lower frequencies. Use your power wisely. These are what bring me joy.

> Music, poetry, spiritual readings, dance, swimming ... *joy!*
> Children playing, family in a park, tennis, golf ... *joy!*
> A view of a mountain, desert, ocean, sunrise, or sunset ... *joy!*
> The last conversation with my parents, grandchildren, lover, or spouse ... *joy!*
> My vocation, career, and colleagues ... *joy!*
> The sun and my precious sunflowers ... *joy!*
> *Choose joy!*

Now, imagine that joy is implanted in your energy body from every joyful experience in this incarnation and your past lives. Ignite this joy from within. Use the power of your intention and imagination to ignite these memories. You are more than your disappointment, regret, guilt, and shame. You are love, and you are loved.

In the energy fields of clients, I envision their past experiences of joy and bring those experiences to their conscious awareness. The joy can get buried in the weight of discordant energy. People who focus on everything that is going wrong and what needs to be fixed miss the imminent joy available. In healing energy sessions, I awaken pockets of light and love. Many clients relate pleasant visions from childhood and their adult lives after the sessions. All is within you; all is available to you from the oneness of the universe too. Choose to fill yourself with the joy available within and beyond.

Every moment in joy has a ripple effect on our energy bodies, building resilience to the ebb and flow of life. Your body responds as though you are there. Your mind is so powerful! Think that you are doing the activity that brings you joy—live it, breath it, and allow the energy to flow through every cell of your body. Whether it is swimming in the ocean, synchronized swimming, playing tennis, or cycling, you can change the electromagnetic charges in your field. Empower you to be *you*!

The following are ways to find joy in your life.

- **Putting yourself first:** Selflessly caring for yourself so that you can selflessly care for others. Do you have a limiting belief that you must always care for others and not yourself? You may not have been taught as a child to put yourself first. Many women of the baby boomer generation are caregivers for their children, spouses, and now aging parents. The caregiver role and weight of the responsibility can take time and energy, leaving no time for self-care. The good news is that you can weave your needs in with the needs of others by prioritizing and caring for yourself so that you have even more energy to care for others.

  You can delegate tasks and not always be available to do a task for others to foster independence. Consider giving your dependents a chance to find their own way in the world by not being so quick to offer suggestions or pick up the phone and start completing the task at hand. Resist the urge to know, to be right, and to be needed in order to feel loved and trust that you are loved. Listen to the soft inner voice of your heart.

  What is the right thing for others? Who really knows? The fact that you think you know what is best for others can be a character trait that you need to let go of in order to focus on yourself. Many of the people who do not know who they are supposed to be or their soul's purpose can get lost in caring for the needs of others. And they should not blame those who become dependent on them if they created the monsters in their life, especially their adult children whose needs still seem to interfere with theirs.

When you put yourself first and focus on what fills you with joy, you can invite in the next phase of your life with enthusiasm, curiosity, and wholeness.

- **Simple acts of kindness:** There is much joy in giving and receiving kindness. When you actually slow down and come out of your important activities long enough to peer into the eyes of another, you receive the gift being offered to you. The simple gesture of someone holding the door open for you can be repaid with the kindness of looking them eye to eye and offering a genuine thank you and a smile.

A smile can bring you joy. Allow the simple joys available to you every day to seep into you. Do not brush them off as unimportant. Every act of kindness has the capacity to shift your world. Even if you are thinking to yourself, *I had the door and did not need the door held for me*, get out of your head and say thank you. I offer that there is a deep flowering that occurs within our spirits in this receiving and a deep satisfaction in being able to see the delight in others when we truly offer our gifts. This exchange of appreciation and sharing can fill a heart with love and open it to joy.

When someone says thank you, what do you do? Do you look them in the eye and say, "My pleasure"? Or do you continue your routine, barely looking back over your shoulder? The opportunity for connection in our world happens every day. Does your cell phone have your attention at dinner while you ignore your family? Maybe you could set a rule—no cell phones at the table. Simple acts of kindness can fill your heart with delight and a knowing of being connected to others.

Can you imagine that you are a gift to someone who loves you and who receives delight in making you happy? This true love does not want anything in return except a smile on your face.

Can you offer a smile? What if you met someone whose pleasure it was to bring joy into your life? How would you receive this offering? If with a heartfelt appreciation and reciprocity of such gifts, your relationship could lead to a long and lasting friendship or partnership. We all want to be appreciated and acknowledged for who we truly are. It validates our uniqueness. This honoring of our unique essence fills us with joy too.

Sometimes we love someone in this very special way but do not receive the smile we desire. In a quiet moment, enter into a deep, still place inside of you and connect to your loved one's heart. What do you find? If you sense a tenderness, know that your love is shared. Not all humans can express love warmly.

It is difficult to sense joy when you are lamenting your mistakes. For example, if you are angry at yourself for pushing your opinion on others and later found out you were wrong, forgive yourself. It is your ego that is based in the physical world and is bruised. You can send those words in a helium balloon and let them float into the sky. All humans make mistakes, so learning to forgive is a key to experiencing joy. It is not always possible in our ever-changing world to be happy. Roll as best you can and remember your blessings.

Imagine a color for joy—make it up. What is your color of joy? Then look at your environment and find the color. You can seek the color everywhere you go and notice how you respond. You will see that there already is joy in your life. When you become curious and seek joy, you shall find it.

A Brittle Clay Heart

A woman came to me for a healing energy session because she was exhausted. Interestingly enough, her name was Joy. She was a beautiful woman with bright eyes and a body that looked physically tired. Joy told me, "I am so tired. I am in my sixties, and I still spend all my time caring for others. I make sure everyone in my life has what they need. I do not have time to take care of myself. I have a beautiful family and do lots of activities with all of them. Yet I feel vulnerable and question if anyone one can truly love me. I don't feel love. My friends tell me how lucky I am. I have an idea of how wonderful love would feel, but I am bewildered by the fact that I cannot feel love."

My intuitive vision revealed a flaky, brittle, clay-like substance around her heart. The field around her heart was like a dried-out terra cotta pot. No life force or love could move in or out without shattering her heart. Dominant masculine energy and a rational mind ran her life without engaging the emotional body of love, nurturing, and nourishment of herself, leading to a compromised heart. She feared that her heart would break if no one loved her, so she kept her heart closed.

I sensed pure light and love within this clay vessel that wanted to be expressed, but fear held it back. I sensed that her family, children, and friends deeply loved and appreciated all that she did for them; it was a genuine sense of love. She acknowledged that she was sure they did love her; she just could not feel it. "There is no joy in my life. I just go through the motions doing the best I can."

Healing energy can be so much fun. I never know what I will see when working with someone. Magic is real—I know that. I used a selenite wand to clear the fear I sensed in her field. It was fear attached to unworthiness and her worry, "What if no one loves me?" I held her heart in my etheric hands and figuratively drew water from the earth to wet and soften the clay surrounding her heart. As the clay dissolved, confetti in all the brilliant colors of the rainbow flew out as though a volcano had just erupted. Streamers of light, love, color, and energy floated into the field around her body. It was magic everywhere; the energy of the room was euphoric.

The expression on her face was priceless. She literally jumped off the table, clicked her heels together, and exclaimed, "What did you do? What just happened?" She was spitting words out of her mouth faster than she could think. "Is this what joy feels like? I want more!"

I showed her how I had used my wand to clear her energy field, demonstrating how she could use it in her life to turn things into joy. She was so excited that I gave her my wand to do her own magic. She can zap worry, fear, and doubt into colorful confetti. The joy was always there. Our intentions can be powerful tools to create magic.

***

The truth is that when we get out of our own way, miracles happens. The deciding factors are not mystical. You have to shift your personal reality through conscious intention and genuine lasting desire, self-acceptance, and love. When you get to know yourself through self-reflection, you can be yourself and follow your own truth. You will never feel fulfilled in life if you create a false self-image that you must live up to. It is time to develop your own ideas instead of ones you picked up secondhand. It is time to be passionate about the things that matter most and pursue an ideal while valuing yourself and your well-being. Illusions can be barriers to joy if you attach to them.

Where do you go for calm? Do you have a special place in your home that you can sit and meditate and enjoy a few sips of tea while it is still hot? What smells do you love—dinner cooking, herbs growing, or an aromatherapy mister of your favorite essential oil? All of these vibrations contribute to your mood.

There is always a place of peace within you; align your vibration to that possibility. Send light to your loved ones. If you sense their resistance to receiving, oh well. Imagine that you become an even finer particle of light that can resonate softly and swiftly through the vapor to where their inner light resides, their true self. Trust that you did just that as you fill their hearts with love.

Your caring for your unique essence of light while in the physical body should be a priority to ease your burdens, to heal your wounds, to bring light to you and your world, and to prepare for a smooth transition into the afterlife. The final task for this incarnation is the life review in the afterlife. A smooth transition can occur if you experience yourself as fully as you can now and make peace with any fear, doubt, resentment, and regrets.

Do not see yourself as struggling to remain alive against all obstacles. See yourself as a river that accepts all change because change is natural as you move from one stage of life to another. Your desires are supported by nature, the invisible world, and the universe—something more than your ego.

Your wisdom can be shared with your children, friends, family, and colleagues as you encourage them to express joy. Then ask them to share their stories of miracles so that others will believe in infinite possibilities and find hope. Can you imagine a world that is vigilant in its efforts to find beauty in nature, people, and simple pleasures? What if we were all one in our desire for peace?

How big is your joy? Add it all up. There is always more to observe than just the sky, sunsets, nature, and the faces of the people in your life. Joy grows when you feed her more. *Choose joy!*

State an affirmation: "I am joy. I choose joy."

Joy is an unbridled experience of universal love. A heart open to the miracle of joy can receive the gift. What would it take for you to be open to receive this gift? What if you believed that joy is always available in the cosmos? Would you choose to access this powerful source of unconditional love and healing? Your reality lies in your beliefs. The truth is that only you can bring joy into your life.

The Summary on Living a Healthy Life

It is time to take all you have learned, set sail on your journey, and incorporate new tools and concepts into your everyday life. This is the moment to bless your experience thus far. Honor yourself for taking the time to honor your mind, body, and soul. Bless your life! Here are some points to remember:

- Your thoughts can create your reality.
- You are a powerful being of light and can change your perception at any moment you choose.
- You have many blessings for which to be grateful.
- All souls are on their own journeys; honor their journeys.
- Nature is always available to ground our spirits.

Many times, when you align with your soul's purpose, you realize that you need to make different choices and leave some people, places, and things behind as you become *you*. Your soul knows that your destiny is unfolding in perfect timing with the divine universe. Trust that you are being supported. You are not alone. As you embark on your new journey, you may meet other like-minded people who share your insights and experiences. No matter how you choose to show up in the world, your contributions are powerful and can change our world.

CHAPTER 21
Sing Your Own Song

For my family, a trip to New York City at Christmas is a tradition. We go to see the tree and lights in Rockefeller Center and to enjoy the hustle and bustle of the city. A visit to Saint Patrick's Cathedral is a must for me so I can light a candle for a family member or friend who is in the need of healing. One year, my son's fiancée, Yashira, spotted a candle to light as she gestured to her son, Adrian, to light the match he had chosen from the tin box. I hesitated as I watched her guide her son in the respectful process to honor her grandfather.

The crowd was thick. The candles flickered, sending a hint of smoke up toward the ceiling, connecting a human prayer to the divine. I waited for a candle to exhaust its flame and surrender its ascent to the arched ceiling of stained glass. A prayer had been heard.

I chose a candle from the hundreds available in the box below the stand that held the blessed offerings. The line formed behind me. I only had time for one prayer, one person for which to light the candle. I thought carefully as I observed the young woman with her son, praying somberly. Many people could use a prayer: my brother-in-law had died a few weeks earlier, my parents and aunts were aging, and a nephew's wife was quite ill. Many people came to mind.

In a flash, my soul cried out, *Pray for me?* The toll of my tumultuous marriage had drained my strength. Selflessly taking a long, slow breath to center and ground myself, I put the money in the tin as I grasped a long, wooden match in my hand. The world was still. This day would be different. I selflessly prayed for myself.

In silence I prayed to release grief and to fill my heart with love for the world. No matter what would come next in my life, I knew that if I had love in my heart, I would be okay. In silence I gazed toward the ceiling of the cathedral and felt grace fill my body. I became lighter at the same time my knees nearly buckled under me. My feet were firmly planted. I was motionless as people swirled around me. I could not hold back the tears from my eyes or the sensation that rose in my chest as it filled with love.

Why had I never prayed for myself? Astonished, I stood in awe as I observed the statues of the saints, the grand oil paintings, the beautiful stained glass, the people visiting from around the world, and the hundreds of lit candles and incense. The cathedral was filled with love. With a silent, motionless pause to take in one more full breath of peace and love, I felt blessed as I hesitantly entered the street. I felt complete and filled with a sense of wholeness, love, and hope, as well as happy to be with my family and friends on this trip.

The next few days, I meditated and reviewed everything in my life that I was completing. I honored what was being left behind to embrace what I was inviting in. My choices on how I spend my time, where I live, what I do for work. and with whom I relate will be more conscious. I am on my own, a solitary light as I was in the church in the midst of so many people with their own prayers, hopes, and dreams—an island in the sea of life. I have the freedom to allow myself to be seen as I am, to be me.

I have the freedom to

- dance
- write
- sing
- travel
- explore
- discover
- laugh
- dream
- be vulnerable
- be me!

What action can you take toward living your life on your terms? You get to decide your expression in the world. State, "I choose to live my life as a conscious human being, I choose to love myself and the world, I choose to (fill in the blank)." For example, you could fill in the blank with any of the following:

- pick more daisies and put them in a glass vase on my dinner table
- walk barefoot in summer
- spend more time with my children, grandchildren, and parents
- wear wild, colorful, flowing skirts and long, sheer blouses
- tell myself I am beautiful
- express the confidence of a twenty-year-old
- laugh at myself more

What would you do more of?

You may have a sense that there is something more that you are seeking in life but you do not know what. It is time to listen to your soft inner voice and to find guidance in the stillness. Can you schedule time to figure out why you do what you do, understand your true nature, and accept what makes you different? Remember that the difference in you is what makes all the difference.

Your soul's story is acted out in real life. It will often draw to you situations, events, or people for transformation. What is true is true; accept what you cannot change. It is inevitable that you will accept your life story, whether in this incarnation or in the afterlife.

There are times when your mind knows you should move on and your emotions keep you in a pattern of "stuckness." Try stepping into the midst of this confusion, but do not overthink. The overthinking can pull you into despair and distract you.

You can befriend the confusion and let go of the resistance. Only then can you discern the truth. Perhaps you can create a passageway in your heart to serve as an escape route for the unrequited emotions. The silver lining is an awakening to your true self. In this moment, be thankful for the wonderful, exuberant expression of you in all your oneness. With full conscious awareness, breathe in this truth.

You can choose to embrace what your life is teaching you, no matter how painful. Your suffering can highlight where you are not yet healed. What if you followed your own beautiful voice? Identify where you lose you power and love yourself more. Trust that you are exactly where you need to be to know what you need to know about *you*. Now you can turn around and tell the story differently as you stand in your power. It is time to sing your own song, dance to your own tune, and find joy in being you.

As you embrace sensuality and beauty, you can live unconditionally according to what makes you happy. The vibrancy of life can fill you with radiance as you share your gifts with others to invite in adventure, travel, new friends, and experiences.

Spirit guides will respond when you ask. Just ask and do not ignore the messages coming to you. The trees, the animals, and the wind can bring messages to you too. You can observe, be curious, and witness your life while keeping your emotions neutral and your overthinking mind quiet. Fly above the earth in your mind's eye and see the big picture. Let the smaller self dissolve into the bigger self.

A sacred space can be created for you to honor the importance of an inner dialogue that recognizes the depth, sensitivities, and creative power within you. It is precisely because you understand that everything you feel, think, say, imagine, or do affects you that you require a practice that helps you return again and again to a place of illumination.

You are a being of light who, with full conscious awareness, chose to be on earth to receive unconditional love and to help our earth star glow brighter in the galaxy. The universe and multiverses will shine brighter too, sustaining our earth for future generations.

Miracles are available to you every day. Embrace them and connect with the people you love in your life. In changing times, we need one another as guideposts to reflect our innermost qualities, to shine our divine light into the world, to foster hope, and to spread the word that *all is well*.

A community of like-minded individuals will deepen your awareness of the world and support you to sing, dance, create, find joy, and inspire you on your journey. Your light is shining brighter today than when you began this journey into the energy and mystical realms. My hope is that you are open to the infinite possibilities in your life and understand there is so much more that you cannot see than you can see.

My stories are meant to support you as you enfold your story, awaken your own healing process, and balance your mind, body, and spirit. They aim to help you trust your own innate wisdom so that you can hear the guidance available to you. You have been chosen by the universe to stand in your power, to shine your unique essence of light, and to be a beacon of light for others.

Thank you for exploring with me what I know to be true of the invisible world of mystery and magic. I am blessed to channel what others need to hear to heal because I was willing to listen and trust. You can too. I have so much more to say about the afterlife, this life, and past lives. Stay tuned for my next book on the multidimensional universe we live in. It will open you to possibilities beyond your imagination to heal, to manifest, and to be you!

You are divine light and come from universal light. Let your voice sing, your love blossom, and the muses in the invisible world help you to be playful and enjoy your journey.

You are a powerful being of light, and all is within you!

Appendix

Who am I? What do I need? What are my gifts? Where I am nurtured? The answers are illuminated in your consciousness as you dive deep into your essence. This appendix contains many practices to support your journey to become you. The most beautiful and meaningful aspects of you will be unearthed so that you can explore vast possibilities in your life. It is time to be *you*!

These practices will keep you on track when chaos enters your life. You become the master of your life, maneuvering through happiness and sorrow. When you allow yourself to be reborn every day, transformation is not only possible but inevitable.

A rebirth means to consciously choose to let the past go, embrace the present moment, and dream of your future. What would it look like? Imagination is the gateway to manifesting your desires. Imagine it and then dream it into reality.

The following is a list of practices.

1. **Connect to your breath:** The breath is the key to calming emotions, clearing the mind, and cleansing the physical body. It is free and always available.
2. **Relieve anxiety:** Anxiety is an electromagnetic charge in your field; it is not you. You are not meant to hold anxiety or destined to be anxious. You can change your reality. This practice releases the excess charge for optimal well-being through grounding to the earth.
3. **Align the hara:** The hara connects your heart center with the earth and the cosmos. An aligned hara is essential to know your soul's purpose and complete life tasks.

4. **Set a healthy energetic boundary:** The biofield that extends beyond your body is a protective cushion that holds your essence at your highest potential. A healthy boundary supports your relationships in the world.

5. **Clear your energy field:** This practice releases discordant charges from your field and resets your protective cushion of love and light.

6. **Balance your chakras:** This practice opens, balances, and connects the spinning wheels of light in your energy system.

7. **Create energetic coherence:** Energetic coherence aligns the physical body, mind, emotions, and soul at the same frequency for optimal health and well-being.

8. **Activate your power within:** This method activates your own inner essence to manifest your desires.

9. **Create a sense of peace and calm**

10. **Read the poem "Children Learn What They Live"**

Now, let's look at these in detail.

1. **Connect to your breath:** *Breath* is Latin for "spirit." Your breath connects your spirit with your higher self and a higher power. A practice to connect to your breath is fundamental and should be done several times a day no matter what is going on in your life.
    - Sit quietly with your head, neck, and back straight. Rest your hands gently on your lap. I invite you to softly close your eyes or gaze at the floor to avoid distraction.
    - On the next breath, say to yourself, "This breath is for me."
    - Then, consciously say to yourself, "I breathe in universal love, I breathe in peace, and I breathe in calm."
    - You mind is a witness to your inhalation and exhalation. Do the best that you can to allow distracting thoughts and emotions to float past you on white clouds. Honor this time to be with your higher self. Remind yourself, "This breath is for me," if you get distracted.
    - Inhale four counts as slowly and as consciously as you can.
    - Hold your breath for two easy counts.

- Exhale for four counts as slowly and consciously as you can.

Continue this breath until you establish a sensation of peace and calm or at least five minutes. You can do this focused breathing whenever you feel stress, tension, mental cloudiness, or anxiety. The breath is an amazing ally for healing. This breathing technique can be helpful before a family meeting, writing a difficult email, going on a trip, easing pain, and anytime you are in a situation that may cause tension.

Gradually, increase your count as you become comfortable with the flow of your breath. You can try to inhale for six counts, hold for three counts, and exhale for six counts. Then inhale for eight counts, hold for four counts, and exhale for eight counts. The goal is to use the breath to be in the moment. The deeper the breath and the longer the count, the deeper you engage your higher self. Yogis who have been practicing this for years may be able to breathe in for twelve counts, hold for six, and exhale for twelve counts. It is not a competition; do what works for you. Every day may be different.

If there comes a time when you feel like your heart has been shattered and needs protecting, be still and breathe in a breath just for you. A slow breath brings you to a deep, still place inside. It is in this place of loving yourself that you will gain a sense of safety, security, peace, and calm. Notice how comfortable you feel to be in your own skin, to be whole, to heal, and to be who you are—all through the magic power of your breath.

2. **Relieve Anxiety:** Once anxiety starts to increase in your field, it can be overwhelming. The more you are aware of the subtle signs of anxiety and what makes you anxious, the better you will be able to manage it.

You can start with the breathing exercise above. Love yourself exactly as you are in this moment. The breath can be enough to cleanse the charge from your system, as you consciously breathe in peace and exhale tension. Be in the present moment and breathe in the love available to you from the universe.

Anxiety is an electromagnetic charge that can be discharged

into the earth. To release these charges, you need to focus consciously on your heart center and imagine energy running down your body and legs, out the bottom of your feet, and into the earth. You do not need to be on the literal ground. It is your intention that is powerful.

- Imagine white crystalline roots flowing from the bottom of your feet and meandering toward the core of the earth.

- Imagine your roots slowly descending into the earth—ten feet, fifty feet, a hundred feet, then a thousand feet or more. Imagine that you are now at the core of the earth. In the loving embrace of Mother Earth, she graciously takes the charge from you. It is here that you are held, loved, and renewed. At the same time, Mother Earth absorbs the discordant energy in your field. This is a great way to discharge anxiety and other emotions. Our bodies are innately wired to release charges into the earth.

- Repeat a mantra: "I am safe in the loving arms of Mother Earth. I am exactly where I am supposed to be."

  If you experience anxiety on a regular basis, reflect on this truth: The bright, unique, glowing light of your spirit shines deep within you and aches to be released into the world. One moment of peace can shift more in your life than you realize. It is simple, really, but it does take effort to create a peaceful life.

3. **Align the hara:** The hara is the line of energy that connects our hearts to the etheric field of the universe and the earth. It is an essential flow of energy for living our souls' purpose. This helps to balance masculine (physical, authority, tasks) and feminine (loving, emotional) energy.

   - Connect to your unique essence of light: Place your left hand on your heart and your right hand on your upper abdomen. Breathe slowly in and out. Allow the breath to be just as it is at this moment in time. There is no need to change anything; just observe. Repeat a mantra of gratitude and feel the gratitude as it moves through your body.

- Connect to Mother Earth: Continue to breathe slowly as you allow, through your mind's eye, to descend into the earth as deeply as you can imagine. Sense the love of Mother Earth surrounding you as though you are in her womb, wanting nothing and needing nothing. All is cared for in this moment.
- When you are ready, invite the light, love, and energy of the earth up your legs and into your body. Sense that you are becoming one with the earth star energy to unconditionally receive the nourishing, nurturing earth energy. This melding with earth dissolves discordant particles in your field and leaves you feeling loved.
- Connect to the cosmos: In your mind's eye, allow yourself to float up from the center of your heart and out of your body toward the ceiling, above the roof, above the clouds, beyond the earth's atmosphere to infinity. When you sense a feeling of pure love, light, peace, and calm, return to your body at the heart center, feeling loved, worthy, and that all is well in this moment in time.
- Clear your mind: Release any discordant thoughts or emotions that may be rocking around in your head. Then invite in the light, love, and energy from the universe to sink into every cell of your body, moving from your head to your toes. Sometimes envisioning the color violet or purple moving through your body will expedite the process.
- Integrate at the heart center: Draw the earth energy from below and the violet light from above into your heart center. Imagine integrating these energies into oneness, connecting your heart energy with universal love.

    At this moment in time, you can feel universal love to heal, comfort, and leave you with the sense that all is well. All is one, and we are all.

4. **Set a healthy energetic boundary:** A healthy energetic boundary is important because it helps to build relationships. Remember that you send and receive information through your energy field. It is necessary to set a healthy boundary to protect yourself from negative energy and hold love in your heart.

- Place your hand on your heart and breathe in peace and breathe in love.
- To clear your field, imagine a plunger of white light moving from above your head down your body. Repeat several times until you feel clear.
- Set your intention to fill your egg-shaped biofield with white light one foot above, below, and around your body. Intentions transform energy into physical form; it is your inherent power. White light is used because it has a high frequency and most people can visualize white light.
- Set the perimeter to be permeable to light and love. This higher frequency of love shields you from lower frequencies of fear. Love and fear cannot be in the same space at the same time.
- Once the biofield is filled with white light, surround your biofield with gold or purple light to seal your field. A second layer of purple light around your biofield protects you from psychic free radicals, external thoughts, and others' egos too. The negative thoughts of people in the environment bounce off the violet light, and your love is sent to them—a win-win!

    If you have trouble visualizing white light, try envisioning sunlight warming your body or fill the space around your body with bubbles, sparkles, roses, butterflies, or whatever raises your frequency so that you can align with your true essence. Replace the shield whenever you feel vulnerable or in a competitive situation, an airport, involved in chaos at work, or any stressful environment. The first thing in the morning is a good time to set your field as part of a daily ritual.

5. **Clear Your Energy Field:** In addition to setting a healthy boundary, the biofield can become charged with psychic free radicals, or negative energy from you and others. Life happens every day. An etheric shower is important to clear your field from time to time, especially before bed and the start of your day.
    - Set an intention to remove discordant particles of light from your field, and then pass your hands over your body from head to toe as though washing your field.

- Imagine that your hands are clearing your field and be sure to cover the entire 360-degree egg-shaped biofield.

A daily practice to set your biofield will provide a protective cushion so that you can respond to events in your life in vibrational autonomy. Meanwhile, this is a process, so every time you notice you are not in vibrational alignment, connect to your heart center and clear your biofield.

6. **Balance Your Chakras:** A daily ritual to balance your chakras can change your life. The following exercise done on a daily basis enhances the immune system, provides mental clarity, heightens intuition, and can release stress that built up during your day. You will sleep better at night too.

- Begin with a gentle, calm breath. Intentionally breathe in love, breathe in calm, and breathe in peace.
- Chakra One: I honor my physical body with nutritious foods, daily exercise, communing with nature, and trust I am safe in my physical world.

   "I am exactly where I am supposed to be at this moment in my life."

- Chakra Two: Today I will experience pleasure in the tasks that I perform. I will trust my emotions and allow them to flow easily through my body. I will enjoy moving my body today in a graceful manner, perhaps swinging my hips and dancing with the flow of life.

   "I trust my emotions."

- Chakra Three: I will stay on track today, ignore the inner critic, and make conscious choices aligned with who I am. I will be aware of when my ego is running the show. I will not lose my power today.

   "I let my inner critic rest, and I embrace my personal power."

- Chakra Four: I will consciously experience the giving and receiving of love and care for myself. I will make sure I have an opportunity to share and receive a kindness toward myself and others. I will be conscious of my breath today.

   "My heart is open to love the world more."

- Chakra Five: I will express my creative self and be confident in my words. I will be conscious and enjoy the sounds I hear in my world today. I will notice how I am received by others. I will speak my words with grace and ease so as not to offend another. I will express my thoughts clearly.

  "I speak with confidence, grace, and ease."
- Chakra Six: I will consciously seek to see beauty in my world today. I choose to receive insights and guidance from within to obtain clarity. I will be free in my thoughts today and mindfully release useless mental chatter. I will notice where I connect with my intuition.

  "I trust my own inner voice."
- Chakra Seven: I will be vigilant to be thankful of where I was blessed today. I will be aware of the divine in all things—nature, people, places, and things. I will be alert for messages and synchronicities in words, people, places, animals, and experiences so that I can be conscious of when the universe is speaking to me.

  "I am divinely guided and protected as the universe aligns the people, places, and things for me to do my best work."

Simply by stating your intention each day, you will notice subtle changes in yourself and the people with whom you interact. Conscious living is contagious, and the more you do it, the easier it is. By simply observing your day, you bring your conscious awareness to where you may make different choices the next day. It is a subtle means to connect to your inner truths.

You can also do a nighttime ritual to review your day without judgment. Intentionally focus your mind on this moment in time. If you observe the mind trying to solve problems or critique your day in any way, return to the breath. Remember, this is you reviewing your day with loving kindness toward yourself and others. In order to be whole and to heal, all the chakras need to be open, balanced, and clear. This exercise will remind you to bless all aspects of your life.

7. Create energetic coherence: Coherence is an energetic state where your mind, body, spirit, and emotions are aligned with your true nature, a state of peace. This process will expand the coherence to your biofield or auric field that is your own radiant protection cushion. Maintaining a frequency of coherence actually creates this field of protection around you so that lower frequencies cannot penetrate your field. Remember the law of attraction? Like frequency attracts like frequency. A higher frequency attracts a higher frequency of like vibrations, keeping you in coherence, peace, calm, mental clarity, and ease. This coherence exercise will clear the biofield around your body by circulating the energy up and out and back down again.

   The ability to create coherence in your energy field and body may seem daunting. Creating coherence requires being in the moment in a kind, loving attitude toward yourself and others, a forgiveness of yourself and others, and letting everything go. If only for a moment you can still your mind, heart, and emotions, you can create coherence and peace. This peaceful moment repeated over and over is how you change your life and heal your body, one moment at time.

   Once in the state of coherence (it may take several minutes), you will discover
   - a sense of heightened intuition and improved health,
   - the ability to release thoughts from your mind, creating mental clarity,
   - resilience to life's challenges and ease in relationships,
   - a release of emotions that could have led to anxiety or stress, and
   - an overall sense of peace.

   The process to create coherence is simple. It takes focus and the desire to be in peace and harmony:
   - Physical body: Touch your heart to engage your physical body. The touch brings your sensations to the heart chakra.
   - Spirit: Breathe in love, peace, and calm. Breathe out that which no longer serves you (thoughts, emotions, illusions from the past or about the future).

- Mind: Invite the mind to repeat a mantra such as "I am" or "I am grateful for my _____" (fill in the blank with something for which you are truly grateful). Repeat the mantra slowly in harmony with your breath.

- Emotion: Feel grateful as you repeat the mantra of gratitude. Feel gratitude through every cell of your body, and fill your biofield with the sense of gratitude.

Allow any discordant thoughts or emotions that come up to float on a white cloud overhead. They are part of your subconscious and will be available later. Be in the moment.

Once you feel a sense of peace and calm, imagine the sensation flowing easily and gently across your chest, down your body, and down your legs into the earth, as deeply as you can allow your energy to flow at this moment in time. Every time may be different. Accept what is right for you in this moment.

From your feet, bring your full conscious awareness up your legs, circulating back up through your body, and returning to your heart center.

Allow this earth energy combined with your heart energy to flow down your arms, releasing what no longer serves you through open palms. And then send the heart energy up and out the top of your head, creating a waterfall of energy around your body.

Once in this state of peace, you can send love, light, and energy to your loved ones and even to your bed and bedroom for a peaceful night's sleep.

8. Activate your power within: Use this practice to clear a limiting belief, thought, or emotion and to heal wounds.

In quiet reflection, identify your strengths. What strengths within you are seeds worth sowing? Each seed is a treasure to be unwrapped and experienced over and over again. Your gifts need to be seen, nurtured, nourished, and exalted. This awareness builds your inner light, strength, and courage to face your wounds, heal, and manifest your desires. This is how synchronicities show up in the physical world. What is happening within us will help create what's happening outside of us.

There are many ways to activate your power within to feel like the powerful being of light that you are. A sacred space can be created—a place to be alone, pray, and activate your divine light. It can be a room where you can also hold sorrow and leave to go back into the world.

As you settle into your sacred space, start with slow, rhythmic breathing to allow your mind and emotions to become calm. Use your imagination to gradually focus on igniting your power within—sense it, hear it, feel it, taste it, and imagine it. Breathe slowly and relax into what it feels like to be in your power. Can you describe the sensations in your body? Do you feel grounded? If so, note to yourself what that feels like.

Continue to breathe slowly and calmly and notice where in your body you sense the energy of this belief. Maybe it is just in your head; just notice. Each part of the body has a different story to tell, and you know yourself better than anyone. Trust what your body is telling you, and create a flow of energy to that part of the body through your conscious awareness while breathing slowly. Then consciously allow your thoughts to become mist as they float out the top of your head. The ego may want to jump in to berate and discourage you, so be mindful and silence the inner critic. You can draw sustenance from your soul and experience humility in the greatness of the universe.

9. **Create a sense of peace and calm:** Guided imagery is used to engage the mind and calm emotions to create a sense of peace. In this state you can connect with your intuition and spirit guides, balance your energy system, and heal your mind, body, emotions, and spirit. You can do this exercise in the morning, at night, or anytime during the day to reset and strengthen your energy field. I suggest that you read this out loud using a voice recorder so you can listen to it later.

   After several days of practicing this exercise, you may no longer need the recording. You can check out this meditation on my website: http://www.kathipickett.com

   The "You Are a Precious Being of Light" guided imagery will bring your full conscious awareness to your divine light. It will remind you of how precious and magnificent you truly are and that you come from a divine, loving universe. You are never alone in spirit.

By choosing to do this exercise, commit to yourself that you will not be distracted. Some options are to silence your phone, dim the lights, hold a healing crystal (such as rose quartz, amethyst, or clear quartz) in your hands, inhale an essential oil (such as lavender, rose absolute, or frankincense), and light a candle to enhance your experience. Honor the time that you are taking for self-care.

Now, I want you to settle in and, with full conscious awareness, breathe in through your nose and out through your mouth several times, each time more and more slowly. Say to yourself, "This breath is for me."

Notice how the full conscious awareness of your breath brings you into this moment and into your body. The frequency of love, peace, and calm already exists in the quantum field. Choose the frequency you want to breathe in with your full conscious awareness.

Breathe in love, breathe in peace, and breathe in calm. And as you exhale, allow any tension in your body to go out with the breath.

Continue breathing slowly and effortlessly, allowing the breath to be as it is. If any distracting thoughts or emotions come up, allow them to go out with the breath.

And yes, for those persistent thoughts that come to you, send them out on a white puffy cloud. They are your thoughts and will come back to you. Do not resist the mind; it is your mind, and as humans, our thoughts will continue. As they float in, allow them to float out. Do not attach to any thoughts or emotions at this time. This is your sacred time and space to connect with your subconscious, spirit, and soul.

At this moment in time, breathe slowly and allow yourself to go to a still, deep place inside.

Now with your full conscious awareness, gently place your hand over your heart, as though you are touching the most precious part of yourself. Take a couple of easy, slow breaths here as you fully connect to your heart.

Observe any sensation in your body with curiosity but no judgment. Perhaps you notice tension or perfect ease in your stillness. Either way, be an observer of your body.

Continue slow, calm breathing. As you breathe and touch your heart, you are connecting your breath with your spirit. Breathe with the intention of connecting to your spirit deep within your heart. Allow any thoughts or the illusions that you have created about your life to go out with the breath.

Now with full conscious awareness invite your mind to repeat a mantra stating what you are truly grateful for, such as, "I am grateful for my life." Repeat this over and over, slowly and intently, so that the mantra and the words are in harmony with your breath.

Slowly state with confidence and clarity, "I am grateful for my life. *I am grateful for my life.*" Say it like you really mean it as you fill your heart center with the emotion of gratitude from deep within your heart. This is your truth; breathe it in. And with the strength from deep within your heart, know that it is true. In this moment, it is your truth. Feel it, sense it, and believe it.

Notice your mind and emotions quieting down as your heart fills with a sense of peace. In this stillness, thoughts can come up from deep within your subconscious. Be kind to yourself and honor this time for your healing. Embrace your thoughts of healing and insight and send the rest out with your breath. Remember, this is your sacred time for healing.

Love yourself in this moment too. Bask in the essence of pure love for yourself. And from your heart center, send the sensation of love easily and gently through your chest, filling your entire chest with love for yourself, love for your life, and love for the world.

Continue sending love through your body as you fill your arms with the light, love, and energy from your heart center. This is your light; it is your love for yourself that you are sending through your body. This is your truth, so with your full conscious awareness allow this light, love, and energy from your heart center to permeate every cell of your body.

As this light, love, and energy flow down your arms, allow them to flow out through your open palms as you release with full conscious awareness and intention that which no longer serves you. Your hands may tingle as energy flows out of your hands and back into the quantum field. Allow this with curiosity; be an observer of you. Imagine your heart center clearing out old beliefs, illusions, guilt, shame, self-doubt. or disappointments from the past that are stuck. You will always remember your experiences; you learn from your past to gain wisdom for your future. Allow any tension to flow out through your hands peacefully.

Now, allow this light, love, and energy from your own true heart to flow down your body and down your legs, through your feet, and into the earth, as deeply as you can allow your energy to flow at this moment in time. Every time may be different, so accept what is right for you in this moment.

Now, allow this light, love, and energy as it flows down your body and out the bottom of your feet to release those particles of light that were embedded in your energy field. You are becoming you—whole, perfect, and complete in your essence and throughout your entire energy body.

As this light, love, and energy are emanating from your own true heart and circulating through your body, now allow this light, love, and energy to flow up through your body and out the top of your head, creating a waterfall of light, love, and energy around your body like a protective cushion. Your egg-shaped biofield is now filled with healing light—feel it and embrace it. This is your field of light; pump it up and expand it with the light, love, and energy from your pure heart.

Now, as you are filled with your own true light, invite the violet ray to flow down the top of your head with its powerful essence of healing. Allow the violet ray to flow down your entire body, filling each and every cell with this healing violet light.

As you now radiate your brilliance within and around your body, state with your full conscious intention to set the perimeter of this field to be permeable to light and love and seal it with gold and purple light to send your love to others whom you may come into contact. This field will neutralize psychic free radicals in your environment, allowing your body to heal in this state of peace and calm. And you will know that all is well.

Imagine the glow from your inner light spreading through your entire body as you become as light as a feather, experiencing the violet light.

You are now attracting more light and love to yourself for healing and emanating light and love to those who you love dearly.

Once in this state of peace, you can send love, light, and energy to yourself, your loved ones, your business, your community, and your home to create a glow of healing light around all you cherish.

May you be at peace with yourself as you are in this moment.

May you be at peace with life as it is in this moment.

May this be your truth in every moment of your life.

Children Learn What They Live

If children live with criticism,
They learn to condemn.
If children live with hostility,
They learn to fight.
If children live with ridicule,
They learn to be shy.
If children live with shame,
They learn to feel guilty.
If children live with encouragement,
They learn confidence.
If children live with tolerance,
They learn to be patient.
If children live with praise,
They learn to appreciate.
If children live with acceptance,
They learn to love.
If children live with approval,
They learn to like themselves.
If children live with honesty,
They learn truthfulness.
If children live with security,
They learn to have faith in themselves and others.
If children live with friendliness,
They learn the world is a nice place in which to live.

—Dorothy Law Nolte

We, too, become what we live. Our thoughts, beliefs, words, and actions become our destiny or fate. Choose your beliefs, thoughts, words, and actions wisely.

Recommended Reading

To develop your intuition:

- Belleruth Naparstek, *Your Sixth Sense: Unlocking the Power of Your Intuition* (San Francisco, CA: Harper Collins Publisher, 2009)

To connect with your spirit guides:

- Sonia Choquette, *Ask Your Guides: Connecting to Your Divine Support System* (Carlsbad, CA: Hayhouse Inc., 2007)

To understand death:

- Elisabeth Kubler-Ross, *On Death and Dying* (Scribner Classics) Classic Edition, (New York: Scribner, 1969). Kübler-Ross first introduced and explored the now-famous idea of the five stages of dealing with death: denial and isolation, anger, bargaining, depression, and acceptance.
- Padma Sambhava and Robert Thurman, *The Tibetan Book of the Dead: The Great Book of Natural Liberation through Understanding in the Between* (New York: Bantam, 1994). The so-called "Tibetan Book of the Dead" has been renowned for centuries as a cornerstone of Buddhist wisdom and religious thought. More recently, it has become highly influential in the Western world for its psychological insights into the processes of death and dying— and what they can teach us about the ways we live our lives. It has also been found to be helpful in the grieving process by people who have recently lost loved ones.
- Elisabeth Kubler-Ross, *Remember the Secret* (Berkeley, CA: Tricycle Press, 2004). This is a beautifully written children's book on what happens when we die.
- Cyndi Dale, *Illuminating the Afterlife: Your Soul's Journey: Through the Worlds Beyond* (Boulder, CO: Soundstrue Inc., 2008). Cyndi Dale describes the energy of death, the twelve planes of light in the afterlife, and their relevance to living a conscious life.

To understand energy medicine:

- Caroline Myss, PhD, *Anatomy of the Spirit: The Seven Stages of Power and Healing* (New York: Penguin Random House LLC, 1996). In this book, Caroline Myss describes the spirit, intuition, and energy medicine in great detail and with great wisdom. This book changed my life, and I continue to refer back to its contents.
- Barbara Brennan, *Hands of Light: A Guide to Healing through the Human Energy Field* (Carlsbad, CA: Bantam Books, 1987). Acknowledgment from Elisabeth Kubler-Ross.
- Anodea Judith, *Wheels of Life: A User's Guide to the Chakra System* (Woodbury, MN: Llewellyn's New Age Series, 1987). Anodea Judith has studied and taught the chakra system for over forty years and describes the energy system in detail.
- Louise Hay, *Heal Your Body* (Author Published, 1984). *Heal Your Body* is a fresh and easy step-by-step guide. Just look up your specific health challenge, and you will find the probable cause for it and the information you need to overcome it by creating a new thought pattern.

Allies for healing our minds, bodies, and spirits

- Essential Oils for Healing
  - Gabriel Mojay, *Aromatherapy for Healing the Spirit: A Guide to Restoring Emotional and Mental Balance through Essential Oils* (London: Gaia Books, 1999. Originally Published by Healing Arts Press, Rochester, Vermont, 1997). *Aromatherapy for Healing the Spirit* presents the first truly comprehensive approach to understanding and applying the psychological benefits of essential oils. The therapeutic and spiritual insights of Oriental medicine help to reveal how aromatherapy works to harmonize the body, mind, and spirit.
- Crystal Healing
  - Robert Simmons and Naisha Ahsian, *The Book of Stones, Revised Edition: Who They Are and What They Teach* (Berkeley, CA: North Atlantic Books, 2015).

- Sharon Whiteley and Ann Marie Chiasson, *Barefoot Wisdom: Better Health through Grounding* (Atglen, PA: Red Feather Mind, Body Spirit)
- Winslow Eliot, *What Would You Do if There Was Nothing You Had to Do? Practices to Create Your Life the Way You Want It to Be* (Published by author, Writespa Press, 2013).

Seeking a Healing Energy Practitioner

Distance healing energy sessions with Kathi Pickett: As an intuitive and healing energy practitioner, I offer distance sessions around the world via Skype, Zoom, and FaceTime. For more information, go to http://www.kathipickett.com for a free consultation or to schedule a session.

Healing Beyond Borders is an organization that trains and supports the development of healing touch practitioners.

Healing Touch is a healing energy modality endorsed by the American Holistic Nursing Association and is a board certification. Healing Touch is a relaxing, nurturing, heart-centered energy therapy that uses gentle, intentional touch that assists in balancing physical, emotional, mental, and spiritual well-being. Classified by the National Institutes of Health as a biofield therapy and nursing intervention, Healing Touch may be used to address the North American Nursing Diagnosis Association (NANDA-1) diagnosis of "Imbalanced Energy Field."

Healing Touch is a collection of standardized, noninvasive techniques that clear, energize, and balance the human and environmental energy fields. Healing Touch assists in creating a coherent and balanced energy field, supporting one's inherent ability to heal. It is safe for all ages and works in harmony with, is complementary to, and may be integrated with standard medical care.

You can find a professional near you on the website: https://www.healingbeyondborders.org

Acknowledgments

This book would not have been possible without my countless friends, family, patients, clients, colleagues and spirits from ancient times to present who have influenced the writing of this book. A big heartfelt thank you and appreciation to the thousands of men and women who have been my teachers as we explored a healing journey together. You are all my noble teachers.

First and most importantly I want to thank my son Jeffrey, my granddaughters Emma-Lee and Mia, my son Michael and his soon to be wife Yashira, her son Adrian and my grandson Lucas. I thank you all every day for being the most important gifts in my life. I cherish our Sunday dinners and every moment you choose to share with me. Time is such a precious gift. I am so thankful to have you in my life.

Secondly, my thanks to my father Garry Meyers, my dear friends Winslow Eliot and Terry Hodur whose attention to detail and insightful feedback was delivered with compassion and grace as the chapters evolved. My father at the age of eighty-eight said he did not understand all of the concepts I was writing about, but he was open to learn more and correct the grammar.

Thirdly, the book could not have been written without the support of my sisters. Bridget's thirst for books as an avid reader of over fifty books a year, Mary's unconditional love and support throughout my life, Brenda's humor and ability to lighten me up, and Aileen's inspiration to reach a wide audience. Thank you for letting me know that I had something worth saying and the confidence to say it.

In addition, I would like to thank a wonderful group of women who I am delighted to know. We formed a group called Kathi's Gathering to support our spiritual growth. The group unanimously ignited my inner scribe. I would like to thank Kathy Souza for her wisdom and compelling support to take a leap of faith. Beth Smith for her loving kindness and fierce truth since the beginning of my journey. She helped to shape who I have become as a healer. And Terry Hodur, Lisa Moriarty, Toni Butman, Karen Coderre, Maria Korny, Diane DeMarco, and Desiree Ducharme for their unwavering encouragement and support. A special thank you for allowing me to be your guide, I am honored to be part of your amazing journey.

And thank you, my dear friends who came into my life, during the time I wrote this book. You filled me with hope. Without your nourishment the writing of the book would not have been possible. You listened to my dreams, offered a safe space for me to vent, release and heal in your loving kindnesses. With the warmest regards I thank Winslow Eliot, Debbie Gray, Susan Braun, and Diane Rossman from the bottom of my heart for welcoming me into their lives and encouraging me to keep going. Your life wisdom and insights are rare and priceless. Your friendship sustained me through difficult times.

A very special thanks to Ann Marie Chiasson, MD author of Barefoot Wisdom who invited me to share in an egg healing ceremony, and a heart initiation at Kripalu. Ann Marie, I appreciate the confidence you gave me to write this book and share my work.

My dear David, my longtime friend and companion who catapulted me into a new version of me. I truly have no idea where I would be if you had not given me the challenge to find my way in the world. Although our separation in the midst of writing the book was painful and distracting. I would not be who I am today. Thank you for being in my life always.

Maureen Skipper, President of Baystate Visiting Nurse Association and Hospice saw something in me that I did not yet see. I am eternally indebted to you for your encouragement at a vulnerable time in my life as I transitioned back into a nursing profession. Maureen is a leader and healer with keen insight into others. She introduced me to Therapeutic Touch sensing that it would resonate with me and my healing energy work began.

A big thank you to my first teacher Sue Andreoli who led me to Ceil Lewonchuk and the Psychic Development Circle early in my studies. And all the reiki girls, Louise Tokman, Denise Williams, Maura Squires, Beth Smith and Carol Jerusik.

And finally, I want to thank Kim Hubbard who gently coaxed me into a relaxed pose beside the peaceful sound of a bubbling river. She said, "Kathi close your eyes and melt into the flow of the river." Then waiting for nature to softly move my hair, she said, "Open your eyes." At that moment she took the photograph for the book. We rescheduled several times as she wanted to get the light just right. Kim, I thank you beyond words for your patience, professionalism and artist gifts.

Last but not least I thank my mother, Jane Meyers who is now in spirit. She would hold my hand and smile up at me after our weekly reiki sessions and tell me how special I am. I still sense her encouragement and love every day.

And, thank you for picking up this book. Please take it, sift it and keep what is worth keeping and with a gentle kiss of kindness blow the rest away.